THE TECHNIQUE AND
SPIRIT OF FUGUE

Dedicated
to
My Wife

GEORGE OLDROYD

THE

TECHNIQUE AND SPIRIT

OF

FUGUE

AN HISTORICAL STUDY

With a Foreword by Sir Stanley Marchant

London
OXFORD UNIVERSITY PRESS
New York   Toronto

Oxford University Press, Ely House, London W. 1

GLASGOW NEW YORK TORONTO MELBOURNE WELLINGTON
CAPE TOWN IBADAN NAIROBI DAR ES SALAAM LUSAKA ADDIS ABABA
DELHI BOMBAY CALCUTTA MADRAS KARACHI LAHORE DACCA
KUALA LUMPUR SINGAPORE HONG KONG TOKYO

ISBN 0 19 317311 5

First edition 1948
Reprinted 1949, 1955, 1960, 1967, and 1971

REPRINTED LITHOGRAPHICALLY IN GREAT BRITAIN
AT THE UNIVERSITY PRESS, OXFORD
BY VIVIAN RIDLER
PRINTER TO THE UNIVERSITY

CONTENTS

CONTENTS

FOREWORD

'The letter killeth, but the spirit giveth life'

D r. Oldroyd's book is based upon this fundamental truth.

He, like many another musician and teacher, has felt the need of a more enlightened understanding of fugal writing; an understanding based, not upon the conflicting statements to be found in text-books, but upon the actual music of the greatest fugal writer of all time.

Authors of text-books and others have found that, after formulating certain rules, difficulties have been encountered particularly when referring to the works of Bach, since his practice does not always conform to these rules. They would seem to have forgotten that the great master was a musician expressing what he felt, not a mechanic working to set formulae.

I commend this scholarly and thoughtful book to all who desire to free themselves from the shackles of such text-books and appreciate more fully J. S. Bach's fugal writing for its sheer beauty of expression.

STANLEY MARCHANT

1947

ACKNOWLEDGEMENTS

I acknowledge my indebtedness

To Messrs. Novello & Co., Ltd. for extracts from *Life of Bach*: Ph. Spitta, translated by Bell and Fuller-Maitland.

To Messrs. Joseph Williams, Ltd. for extract from *Studies in the Art of Counterpoint*, Stewart Macpherson.

To Messrs. Constable & Co., Ltd. for extracts from *Johann Sebastian Bach*: J. N. Forkel, translated by C. Sanford Terry.

To Messrs. Augener, Ltd. for extracts from *Fugue* by Ebenezer Prout.

To Messrs. MacMillan & Co., Ltd. for extract from *Counterpoint and Harmony* by Sir E. C. Bairstow.

To Messrs. J. Curwen & Sons, Ltd. for extract from the Preface to *Purcell Fantasias*, edited by Peter Warlock and André Mangeot.

To Professor E. J. Dent for extracts from his privately printed *Notes on Fugue*.

To the University of London for extracts from Examination papers.

To the Oxford University Press for extracts from the following books:

D. F. Tovey, *Musical Textures*, and *A Musician Talks*.

C. Sanford Terry, *Bach—The Historical Approach*.

Cecil Gray, *The Forty-eight Preludes and Fugues of J. S. Bach*.

R. O. Morris, *The Structure of Music*.

J. H. Arnold, *Plainsong Accompaniment*.

C. H. Kitson, *Elements of Fugal Construction*.

I record

My gratitude to E. Stanley Roper, Esq., C.V.O., M.A., Organist and Composer to H.M. Chapels Royal, St. James's, for friendly interest and counsel.

My thanks to C. Wakelin Scott, Esq., B.A., and to Kenneth Eade, Esq., L.R.A.M., F.T.C.L., A.R.C.M., for valuable help in proof-reading.

My appreciation of untiring assistance given to me by my son Michael and my daughter Linnet Mary during the course of preparing the book for the Press.

GEORGE OLDROYD

PREFACE

The fugues of John Sebastian Bach are so many masterpieces in the realm of Music. Each one is a new and particular creation, for each has its own design, inspired by the character and mood of the subject. Thus, as Bach teaches us, a fugue is not a thing made to fit into a mould called fugue-form, but a thing whose order of growth is inherent in its subject.

In his own way—his own perfect way—he blended counterpoint and harmony as no one else had done and created works of sublime expression. One might reverently say he breathed into Fugue and gave it a Spirit. To me Bach's '48' are an embodiment of Truth.

This book is not a study of fugal composition, that is, EXPRESSION through the medium of fugue, though it might perhaps be called a prelude to such study, for it is largely concerned with the technique of writing. But it is a book which, one hopes, may arouse the young earnest musician to deep contemplation of Bach's works, so that he may draw from them wisdom and understanding such as will guide him in his own endeavours whether he be creator, performer or interpreter. It has also the express purpose of equipping students for the tests in the writing of Fugues as demanded by Diploma and University Degree Examinations, and its design has been influenced by this. Such tests are intended to afford proof of the student's ability to handle well, and to good purpose, the contrapuntal devices commonly associated with fugal writing. A coherent fugue of appropriate texture should be produced even though it may not be an example of composition in fugue. Now Bach's fugues are composition in fugue, and by sheer skill and wisdom Bach has given us almost as many forms as fugues. We find that a fugue may evolve without calling into play all available contrapuntal means—perhaps concentrating on one only, as is more or less the case in the C major fugue, Vol. I of the '48.' In other words each fugue does not attempt to exhibit the whole cycle of contrapuntal devices, nor to fit into the same mould. For this reason the student who seeks his 'model' of fugue-form from the '48' is apt to become puzzled and produce unconvincing work. He neither creates a fugue attaining the level of composition in the Bach sense, nor provides evidence of sufficiently varied skill in contrapuntal device. He needs guidance. Nevertheless Bach is the master to whom he must go and from whom he must learn the scholarship and art of fugal technique.

PREFACE

Experience as teacher and examiner has convinced me that fugue-writing probes the armour of the student as no other test, and that it is the least gripped of all his studies. Innumerable examples that I have seen have created the impression that many students have worked with very hazy ideas as to what they were aiming at. I am also convinced that writing in fugue has a vitalizing effect upon practical playing no less than upon creative endeavour. The study of Bach's work is fertilizing to the mind which is ready to absorb its technique and spirit. It develops alertness and freedom of mind musically, and as surely brings about a sober judgment regarding mathematical exactness. This last-mentioned is often taken for a virtue which must be maintained always, no matter at what price. But indeed it may prove to be a snare, killing the spirit that would raise the fugue above the commonplace.

The suggestions in the following pages are not claimed to be exhaustive or the only ones; they are merely a contribution to the study of a subject which, to the student at least, has been surrounded by prickly hedges. The suggestions are based upon a long and close intimacy with the methods and traditions of pre-Bachian composers and Bach's fugues, no two of which are alike either in construction as a whole or in the devices employed. It is unlikely that any fugue of Bach corresponds in detail to the schemes mapped out herein. His fugues unfold in a bewildering variety of ways.

A great hindrance to good contrapuntal work is poor harmonic basis. The power to choose chord progressions well—in a word, clear harmonic-thinking—is the first essential. Weakness in this respect is too often an unsuspected cause of trouble.

'Texture' is a word frequently to be met with in the course of this book. Now texture is a weaving of some kind whether we think in terms of Harris tweed or music. The weaving idea is its very character; so it is that fugal writing must be dominated by the textural habit of thought. Counterpoint in music is the power of expression in accordance with this way of thinking; in fact I have heard it said that this is even the Art of Composition. If we consider the sister arts of Painting and Sculpture we see the force of this. Their power to satisfy depends essentially on harmonious linear relationship.

Every fugue subject or thread offers its own scope for textural thought, suggests its own design for the weave.[1] Every completed fugue is therefore a particular work. There is no such thing as fugue-form in the usually

---

[1] Forkel relates that: 'Bach was fond of listening to the music of other composers. If he and one of his elder sons happened to be in a church when a fugue was played, directly the subject had been stated he always pointed out how it ought to be developed.'

2

accepted sense and meaning of the word form in music, which is a plan or structure broadly fixed.

Considerable space is devoted to what the late Sir Donald Tovey called 'vexatious minutiae about the relations between subject and answer'. I hope it is not space ill-used, and that the contribution that I have made may help some little towards the elucidation of a tantalizing problem.

Along with the study of the technique of fugue the student's mind is drawn to something inseparable from it which I call the Spirit of fugue; this is exquisitely shown forth in the workmanship of Bach and is the quintessence of artistry. I can think of no name whereby to call it other than spirit. In my opinion this aspect of Bach's work has great significance, particularly of a poetic kind. That it must affect quality of performance or interpretation is obvious.

I hope the short chapter concerning Bach and Fux may set the student thinking.

Distinguished writers have found it difficult to explain satisfactorily many excerpts from Bach's fugues. Prout in his book on Fugue (Augener) wrote:

'There is probably no branch of musical composition in which theory is more widely, one might almost say hopelessly, at variance with practice than Fugue. Bach's fugues are the finest in existence. . . . Bach is treated as the final authority.'

With this statement I entirely agree; were it not so I should not have written this book.

Prout also says:

'Whatever Bach does systematically and not merely exceptionally is the correct thing for a student to do.'

I would go further and say that we should so know Bach's mind as to realize that he did the *right* thing.

In certain instances Bach's procedure has been regarded as exceptional, and has been criticized as 'showing no consistency in the matter', 'seems to have confused the issue' and so on. But I would be so bold as to assert that Bach's mind was too great and clear to be confused. His work gives proof of profound scholarship; he was no mere theorizer.

It is essential to be able to explain whatever one, to whom we refer as an authority, does. It is hoped that a clearer understanding of Bach's ways will be possible in the light of considerations and conclusions put forward —it is believed for the first time—in the following pages.

PREFACE

I am convinced, however, that if we cannot explain Bach, we must look for the confusion in our own minds and not in his.

Finally may the student be encouraged to explore the possibilities of Composition in Fugue. In the eighteenth century Bach gave the world immortal music of this kind. It has been said that the twentieth century needs another Bach.

GEORGE OLDROYD

1947

A NOTE ON TERMINOLOGY

I have endeavoured throughout to avoid the use of the phrase 'invertible counterpoint' and cognate expressions. To 'invert' means to turn upside-down, and it seemed to me misleading, at any rate in this book, to employ the word in order to describe the transfer of one strand of counterpoint *as it stands* to another voice—which is what so-called invertible counterpoint implies. There is usually no question of real inversion of material, and I have therefore substituted in preference the phrases: 'interchangeable counterpoint', 'interchanged version' or 'interchange', etc. Where the word inversion does appear, it will be found to be used in its strict sense.

SOME HISTORICAL OBSERVATIONS

Cecil Gray mentions on page seven of his book, *The Forty-eight Preludes and Fugues of J. S. Bach,* that 'the amount of latitude that Bach permits himself, incidentally, may be gauged by the fact that none of the recognized authorities who have written treatises on the subject—such as Fux, Albrechtsberger, or Cherubini—ever even mentions him'.

I would add to Fux (1660-1741), Albrechtsberger (1736-1809), and Cherubini (1760-1842), another writer, Marpurg (1718-95), who also did not deign to refer to Bach's methods or works in the treatise he published in 1753, which was a summary of the whole science of Counterpoint at that period.

The first volume of Bach's 'Forty-eight' was completed in 1722, and as Fux's treatise appeared (in Latin) in 1725, it is possible, though doubtful, that Fux was not acquainted with it.

Marpurg, however, lived for forty-five years after Bach's death in 1750. He came into personal contact with Bach and, according to the late Dr. C. S. Terry, praised the technical mastery of Bach's *Art of Fugue*, but nevertheless was silent about it in his up-to-date publication of 1753. It would appear, too, that some time after Bach's death there was a musical controversy between Marpurg and one of Bach's pupils named Kirnberger. Marpurg, irritated by Kirnberger's constant quoting of his master, angrily exclaimed that no one would ever be persuaded that Bach would have expounded the principles of harmony according to the views of Kirnberger. Marpurg felt sure that, if there existed any instructions on harmony in the handwriting of Bach, they would not be found to contain only that which Kirnberger put before them as Bach's way of teaching.

We learn from Kirnberger that Bach considered it best to begin with four-part counterpoint, on the grounds that it was impossible to write good two- or three-part counterpoint until one was familiar with that in four parts: for as the harmony must of necessity be incomplete, anyone not thoroughly acquainted with four-part writing could not decide with certainty what should be left out of the harmony in any given case.

Now Kirnberger, we are told, revered his master too much to make false statements about his ways of teaching. Furthermore we find that he is supported by Dr. C. S. Terry who says about Bach's method that:

'omitting theoretical counterpoint, he started his pupils forthwith on

5

four-part harmony providing a figured bass for their transliteration. He required them to write each part on a separate stave, in order that each should receive a definite melodic form, and also be clearly followed in relation to the parts above and below it. When his pupils' knowledge had progressed sufficiently, he introduced them to counterpoint, and within limitations allowed them unusual liberty. Consistency of expression, variety of style, rhythm and melody were the qualities he called for.'

After reading the above one is constrained to believe that Bach's ways did not fit in with the ideas of Fux and Marpurg. Little wonder that in spite of Marpurg's praising the 'finished article' (as in his reference to the *Art of Fugue*) he did not feel disposed to recognize or incorporate Bach's method of teaching in his treatise on counterpoint (1753).

It seems strange too that Albrechtsberger (from whom Beethoven had some lessons) and Cherubini should have been content to reiterate the theoretical rules of Fux. Could they be ignorant of Bach's work? Was the Italian academic hierarchy determined that Bach should remain local, soon to pass into oblivion? Had even the Mendelssohn revival of Bach's 'Passion' in 1829 been unheeded by Cherubini whose *Counterpoint and Fugue* was not published till 1833?

In the preface to that book Fétis refers to the examples 'as models of that perfection of style that distinguishes the productions of the ancient Italian masters'. Obviously, attention was focused on the ideas of Italian origin only—there was no room to display or consider others—Bach's were not to be countenanced.

Apropos of this we find Prout saying very plainly that:

'with regard to Fugue there are few indeed of the old precepts which are not continually, not to say systematically, violated by the greatest masters. Reason for this is no doubt that the standard authorities on the subject, Fux and Marpurg, treated it from the point of view of the seventeenth century, and that most of their successors such as Albrechtsberger and Cherubini (to name two of the most illustrious) have in the main adopted their rules *taking little or no account of the reformation, amounting almost to a reconstruction, of the fugue at the hands of J. S. Bach.*'

Nor can I refrain from quoting at this point from Sir Donald Tovey's book, *A Musician Talks*:

'The rules of fugue as an art-form have been drawn up mostly with regard to the sole convenience of teachers and with no regard whatever to the practice of classical composers, except, paradoxically enough, in certain vexatious minutiae about the relation between subject and answer. *As the rules were drawn up by teachers to whom Bach was either unknown or an object of strong disapproval, this is perhaps not surprising.*'

But, surprised as we may be to learn of the attitude or ignorance of the above musicians concerning Bach, we can be no less astonished at the un-informed mind of our own historian, Dr. Burney, concerning him. But it must suffice that the reader be referred to the letters of that learned and discerning musician Samuel Wesley[1] for enlightenment on this matter. It was he who discovered the greatness of Bach and preached it in this country—and revealed Burney's comparative ignorance of Handel's con-temporary. It is amazing that one so travelled as Dr. Burney should be so little aware of J. S. Bach.

Bach was not only a colossus of a composer; he was the musician's highest example of a teacher, for he was a clear-minded scholar, a pro-gressive thinker. He was thoroughly acquainted with the great contra-puntal works of the sixteenth century and knew the Italian school of that period as well as of his own day (see the list of works in the choir library of St. Thomas's, Leipzig, as mentioned by Dr. C. S. Terry). He perceived the true spirit of Counterpoint unfettered by harmony, and expressed it in terms of his own music as truly as did Palestrina. He knew it meant freedom of melody, beauty of curve in sound, as free from metrical im-positions as Plainsong. He regarded MELODY as the QUEEN whose privilege and age-long right of freedom should always be retained by her, and recognized by HARMONY the KING.

Study his music and you will discover this on every page.

The Italian post-Palestrinian School, dating from the Neapolitan School of Opera, broke away from the counterpoint of the motet and madrigal in search of new means of expression, more suited to the new ends, and produced a new *harmonic counterpoint*. This type created movement, but it ran between metrical and harmonic shafts to which it was harnessed. Though smooth and mellifluous, it lost much of the subtlety of the original melodic art, which we may call Italian, the art of St. Gregory. In Handel, Haydn and Mozart we see the highest work of this post-Palestrinian School of Italy.

Bach created a new school, or rather developed an old one. His contra-puntal thought is the spirit and freedom of Plainsong, *melody flying free*; and this he infused into 'parts in combination', creating music possessed of a daring and boldness not experienced by Italian ways. It was *new*. It could be as tenderly expressive as it could be powerfully virile. The clashings, the momentary jarrings, are the feature, the gift, the *price* if you will, of melodic freedom truly pursued.

[1] See "The Bach Letters". Samuel Wesley (Wm. Reeves, 1878).

SOME HISTORICAL OBSERVATIONS

Forkel[1] in his book on Bach states that 'from the year 1720 until his death in 1750 Bach's harmony consists in this melodic interweaving of independent melodies so perfect in their union that each part seems to constitute the tonic melody. Even in his four-part writing we can, not infrequently, leave out the upper and lower parts and still find the middle parts melodious and agreeable. . . . But in harmony of this kind each part must be highly plastic; otherwise it cannot play its rôle as an actual melody and at the same time combine with the other parts. *To produce it Bach followed a course of his own upon which the text-books of his day were silent*, but which his genius suggested to him. Its originality consists in the freedom of his part-writing, in which he transgresses, seemingly at any rate, rules long established and to his contemporaries almost sacred.'

The Italian Counterpoint as we see it in Handel is said to run as smooth as velvet. True indeed, but it needs a master of Handel's calibre to prevent it from producing dullness and insipidity. It is associated with a thing— the Opera—created to please and entertain a gay Italian people, a pleasure-loving people. In contrast, Bach's counterpoint is associated with a deep, religious expression, and it turned to the fount of religious expression, Plainsong, for its inspiration.[2]

Here lies the difference between the two. Both have their purpose. Bach knew well the Italian style, and used it when he wished; but the Italians undoubtedly eschewed his style, and their theorists, so-called authorities, ignored it. This leads us, however, to a sphere quite beyond the confines and purpose of this book, but one of deep musical significance and as yet almost untouched by our teaching methods.

[1] *J. S. Bach* by J. N. Forkel (translated into English from the German by C. S. Terry, Litt.D.)—Constable.

[2] Cecil Gray says, 'In some numbers (of the Forty-Eight Preludes and Fugues) we feel the pull of the tradition which goes back through Palestrina to the Netherlanders, and from them to the Gregorian Chant itself, the fountain-head of all European music.'

FUX AND BACH

There can be little doubt that Fux, in writing his treatise, *Gradus ad Parnassum* which appeared in 1725, was earnestly endeavouring —according to his own views—to provide a corrective to the deterioration of part-writing which had set in since the advent of the 'New Music', and which characterized his own period. One may be quite at fault in surmising that Fux attributed to his methods nothing beyond a corrective influence; but it seems reasonable to regard as possible that he understood his precise purpose and its limitations more exactly than did those who came after him and who adopted his counsels as the basis of a school of composition. Such a school had little in common with Bach beyond the high purpose of restoring the art of good part-writing, for Fux's ways were not Bach's ways; the two methods sprang from totally different sources and produced different results. A Bachian Chorale treatment could not have come to pass by Fuxian technique. It may be worth while, in the student's interest, if a brief outline of these affairs is sketched out.

Bach and Thorough-bass

According to Spitta (Volume III, page 123), Bach founded his teaching of Composition on the knowledge of Thorough-bass.

> 'In the year 1624, the Berlin Cantor, Johann Cruger, calls this method which he himself employed, a well-known one; and although for a time it held less prominence than various other methods which he describes, it is certain that it never died out again, but that, like practical music itself, it waxed stronger and stronger, and, in Germany at least, gradually became the prevailing method. Thus in employing this method Bach did nothing new, for it had been long in use. (Spitta, Vol. III, p. 118 *et seq.*).

. . . .

> The short rules of thorough-bass which Bach noted down for his wife, Anna Magdalena, in her later clavier book are all that has hitherto been known of this method. There exists, however, a more elaborate work on thorough-bass by Bach, *Principles of thorough-bass and directions for performing it in four-parts in accompanying, for his scholars in music.*'

Bach calls thorough-bass the beginning of composition, adding that:

'if anyone who is willing to learn can take in thorough-bass and imprint it on his memory, he may be assured that he has already grasped a great part of the whole art.'

Spitta writes further:

'The great importance attached by Bach to a knowledge of thorough-bass, not only for the purpose of accompanying, is confirmed by other evidence. . . . Bach was accustomed to lead his advanced pupils up to the point of making extempore accompaniment, even to independent pieces of music, by means of figured bass and a few other indications.'

.   .   .   .

'In a preparatory instruction book for composition such as this is, it seems evident that Bach should in his actual teaching have preferred the method which leads straight, after treating intervals, to chords, chord-combinations, and modulations, and after that, too, not to begin with two-part counterpoint, but with simple counterpoint in four parts.'

Bach's reason for this has already been stated, but it is worth while repeating it (Spitta, Vol. III, p. 121):

'it is best to begin with four-part counterpoint as it is impossible to write good two- or three-part counterpoint until one is familiar with that in four parts, for as the harmony must necessarily be incomplete, one who is not thoroughly acquainted with four-part writing cannot decide with certainty what should be left out of the harmony in any given case.'

Spitta continues:

'This rule is based on the principle that all combinations of notes which can be placed in juxtaposition are to be referred to, or connected with, certain fundamental harmonies—the only principle adopted in musical practice even so early as the seventeenth century. Bach's compositions take it for granted—the boldness and freedom of his part-writing, polyphony and modulation, his way of resolving chords by the interchange of parts, and even his occasional overstepping of all generally held rules of composition are always limited by this "harmonic" theory, which is developed to such an astounding degree of certainty that he could dare even the boldest flights.'

Further, Spitta writes:

'We cannot suppose that simultaneously with the music of the seventeenth century, the theoretical branch of the subject developed in proportion. . . . So much however is certain that there were practical musicians even at the beginning of the seventeenth century who knew that the easiest introduction to the art of composition was the knowledge of thorough-bass. Of course it had its weak points and was liable to misuse and superficial treatment in unskilful hands. On this account it was assailed in 1725 by Fux (capellmeister at Vienna) with his *Gradus ad Parnassum.*'

Fux's attack on Thorough-bass

'In this (*Gradus ad Parnassum*) he begins the course of composition with simple two-part counterpoint note against note, and after a thorough working out of the five kinds[1] of simple two-, three- and four-part counterpoint, he proceeds gradually to imitation, to fugue in two, three and four parts; he next treats double counterpoint, applying the same again to fugue, and concludes with some chapters on the church style and recitative, thorough-bass remaining unnoticed.

'This method (states Spitta) was really new at that time in certain circles and Fux designated it as such; nor does he attempt to conceal the reactionary spirit which led him to oppose the increasing arbitrariness and lawlessness in music. In fact, it was only a revival and completion[2] of the musical teaching of the sixteenth century, and refers only to unaccompanied vocal music in the polyphonic style, and Fux wished this to be regarded as the starting point of all musical education.'
Continuing, Spitta says:

'As a matter of fact there was much more sympathy between Bach and Fux than might at first appear. With regard to the development of the art in Germany, it must not be thought that up to Bach's time a strictly contrapuntal method prevailed and that Bach introduced a freer style. A more exact examination of the German composers, particularly those of the latter half of the seventeenth century, and among them notably the organ and clavier masters who were the glory of that period, will show plainly that the opposite is the case. Awkwardness in polyphonic vocal writing had much increased during the century, and even the authorized freedom of instrumental composers threatened to

[1] How and on what basis Fux devised these five kinds of simple counterpoint is not discussed.

[2] Spitta here seems to suggest that Fux devised these five kinds of simple counterpoint from sixteenth-century technique. But I would ask—could Palestrina be imagined as instructing his pupils in this manner? As to its being a revival and completion of sixteenth-century teaching, these are claims that I do not think could be substantiated—sixteenth-century teaching had no need of completion— —it was to be seen in perfection in the compositions of Palestrina, and its revival could best be brought about by the study of those compositions, not by donning a Fuxian straight-jacket.

degenerate into arbitrary laxity. Only to a very limited degree can Bach be said to have inherited from his predecessors his astounding contrapuntal skill and the strictness and purity of his style.

'He re-introduced these qualities (strictness and purity of style) into the art with a leaning indeed towards the old classical models, but following rather the leading of his own genius. Through him the old approved rules of part-writing again came to be duly honoured, with such modifications, it is true, as were rendered by the alteration in the tone-material, and it was Bach who once more taught the organ and clavier composers to write as a rule in real parts and to keep the same number of parts throughout the whole piece.'

'Hence (says Spitta), notwithstanding his approval of Fux's method it was only natural for Bach to prefer another style of instruction.'

From this outline of the historical situation by Spitta it is clearly seen how both Fux and Bach endeavoured to serve the cause of music, but whereas Fux refers only to unaccompanied vocal music, Bach refers both to vocal and instrumental. Bach taught simple counterpoint by giving a chorale melody to be harmonized in four parts; thus his teaching had a vocal beginning, but even from the starting-point it was of a different stamp from Fux's counterpoint; it was of a more pregnant calibre. Bach's pupils were taught thorough-bass not at first extempore, but by writing out four-part accompaniments to Albinoni's Violin solos, from the bass part. The chorales of Bach are models of four-part writing and are the essence of the art of counterpoint applied to the harmonic art as contrasted with the canonic or imitational type of polyphonic composition. Thus Bach's teaching was at the same time both vocal and instrumental. It was grounded upon a harmonic system and yet the true spirit of the contrapuntal art was preserved. In a word Bach took counterpoint in all its freedom and beauty and grafted it upon the harmony of his era. This was indeed one of Bach's greatest achievements.

Dr. C. S. Terry (in *Bach, The Historical Approach*) says:

'But till he (Bach) expounded it by rule and example, the Fugue was a contrapuntal soulless exercise. Among its masters Bach had regard for Fux whose *Gradus ad Parnassum* published in 1725 was a standard manual. But in Fux's hands the fugue was a mechanical and lifeless exercise.

'"First choose a subject suitable to the key you intend to compose in," he directs, "and write it down in that part in which you propose to begin. Then repeat the subject in the second part, either at the interval of the fourth or fifth, adding such notes in the first part as will agree with it . . ." and so on with the prosaic precision of a cookery book!'

PRE-BACHIAN COMPOSITION IN FUGAL MANNER

A consideration of examples of composition in the fugal manner prior to the time of Bach may help the student towards a clearer idea of how Bach's predecessors had been working, also assist him in realizing what Bach had to contend with and what he achieved when he presented *fugue in all its diversity* as a perfect art-form, and revealed the ideal towards which all previous efforts had been tending.

I have chosen for our purpose two works by a great forerunner of Bach, namely, Frescobaldi (1583-1643), whose contributions to instrumental music as represented by his Canzonas and Fugues show him to be a musician of deserved eminence. Before proceeding to the detailed examination of these two works, it may not be out of place to make one or two general observations which a mere glance at some twenty-five Canzonas of Frescobaldi brings forth.

The key-signatures are confined to the natural or one flat—in fact, the first Canzona retains the modal signature of one flat although finally a cadence in G minor (with tierce de picardie) occurs, showing that it is in the Dorian mode transposed. None of them can be regarded as key-signatures in our modern sense. This restriction of Mode or Key was in keeping with the old system of keyboard tuning—the unequal temperament system, which allowed of perfect intonation within an orbit of a few closely related keys. This reminds us of the purpose of Bach's first volume of the '48', for it set Bach's seal upon the equal temperament system of tuning, and provided compositions written in all the twelve major and minor keys. The Canzonas show clearly the struggle going on to create a composition of any *length*, mainly on contrapuntal lines. (This business of creating pieces of any *length*, is one of the most important that composers have had to explore. Unfortunately students meet it under the name of 'Form in Music', and never get an appetite for it, or soon suffer from indigestion, and leave it severely alone unless driven to it by the demands of some coveted diploma.)

(i) CANZONA by Frescobaldi.

The following notes on this will place something definite in the student's mind as to what kind of composition preceded Fugue. This Canzona is in the Dorian mode transposed.

It is a succession of five short sections, varying in time-signature and tempo, all showing simple contrapuntal devices, each section unrelated materially to the others. There is no expansion of a single theme, no important organic growth, no reappearances of the theme in keys or at pitches other than the Tonic or Dominant. The following analysis takes each section in turn; all sections played one after the other give the Canzona complete; this illustrates the state or stage of harmonic feeling at this period—strongly modal yet foreshadowing modern key-tonality as at the perfect cadences:

Analysis.—The Subject begins on the dominant note. It follows again immediately—then in bars 3 and 4 the Answer appears twice in succession. This procedure is not usual in later fugal work. There are two more successive appearances of the Subject and one of the Answer coming to a full close on the tonic chord G with tierce de picardie, after which the Answer appears twice in succession, followed by the Subject which ends the section on a major chord of the tonic G with a perfect cadence. The last two appearances of the Answer have a counterpoint against them and *above* them. This counterpoint appears against the final entry of the subject but *below* it, thus providing a short example of double counterpoint.

Analysis.—This consists of nine bars in $\frac{3}{4}$ time Grave, showing free imitation of a short rising group of notes ⌐————. The imitative entries are not at regular distances until bar 6 is reached, when they occur at one bar's distance. The section ends (as Section 1) with a perfect cadence and tierce de picardie in G. Without a break the music moves on to:

Analysis.—Four voices take part in imitative work, sometimes combining two short ideas and showing them in double counterpoint (as in bar 2), sometimes one idea (as in bar 4). This section reverts to quaver and semiquaver movement. It concludes on a tierce de picardie again on a chord marking a long repose—the first one since the beginning of the Canzona.

Analysis.—Now begins Section 4, as a period of eight bars (overlapping Section 4a) marked *sostenuto* and resorting to crotchet and quaver movement akin to Section 2. Two ideas, *a* and *b*, appear simultaneously, work themselves quite simply to a close in the eighth bar, where we have a full close in D minor but with tierce de picardie. For the first time this full close in the tonality of the Answer appears with any degree of cadential feeling.

The next six bars which I have marked Section 4a return to the common time and to some extent the manner of movement in quaver and semiquaver of Section 1. But it is marked 4a because the figure *b* is the same as figure *b* in Section 4, in a diminutive form. The section ends with a plagal cadence in the tonality of the answer.

Analysis.—This is called Section 5 because its purpose seems definitely to be the providing of a climax, a winding-up. But its material really makes it *4b*, as the first four crotchet notes are the same as those of Section 4 (figure b) and the same as the figure *b* in Section 4a. In other words, Sections 4, 4a, and 5 might be grouped together as they spring from the same figure. It will be seen that the figures *b* and *c* appear mostly together, though occasionally they appear the one without the other. The material is used in double counterpoint fashion and with considerable freedom and ingenuity.

This full Canzona gives a fair idea of a work based on contrapuntal material (but not a Fugue) by a master of the period about a century before J. S. Bach.

Now let us consider a Fugue.

17

Analysis.—The above is the Exposition of the Fugue. It is obviously conceived in a key and not a mode—there is no trace of modal tonality—and definitely it is G minor. The subject is more extensive than that of the Canzona (only one bar) and remains in the key of the Tonic G minor.

The subject is answered in the dominant minor (differing from the Canzona which repeated the subject in the tonic).

The counterpoint against the Answer has character and purpose, and makes good two-part harmony and texture with the subject.

The ending of the answer does not adhere strictly to the subject—it is somewhat free.

Bars 9 and 10 form a Codetta between the Answer and the next appearance of the subject. It is an example of sequential workmanship derived from ⌐ a ¬, the closing fragment of the counterpoint, or *counter-subject*.

N.B.—A counterpoint against the subject is not termed counter-subject unless it appears with the subject systematically, but I prefer to use the term counter-subject whether appearing systematically with the subject or not. Prout says, 'If this counterpoint is intended for subsequent use it *must* be written in double-counterpoint.' This is an important observation.

In the latter half of bar 14 will be seen the Answer in the Bass, in which voice the Subject last appeared. A little later the Subject appears in the Treble (in Tonic key) so that these two entries may be regarded either as redundant entries, or as a counter-exposition.

Episode I

Following this counter-exposition one expects an Episode, and what may be regarded as an Episode occurs in an interesting way. It appears as follows:

Subject in full, in C minor

Analysis.—The Answer (D minor) begins, but the second bar of it x⌐▬▬▬⌐ is repeated twice sequentially. This same germ x⌐▬▬▬⌐ is similarly treated in bars 6 and 7 where an extra voice steals in, making four for the time being, and then disappears at bar 9. (This convenient procedure happens again.)[1] Although this section begins with the theme of the Fugue, yet it may be regarded as an episode in which a fragment from the theme is pursued with a new purpose. One can hardly say that it serves the purpose of modulation to the key of the next thematic entry in C minor at bar 8, at any rate in a manner that could be regarded as orthodox, for in bar 7 F major is touched and at the beginning of bar 8 is the C major chord or dominant in F, which is merely changed to C minor chord on the third beat of bar 8. From that point the theme proceeds in the tonality of C minor.

Middle Entry in Sub-dominant Minor Key, and Episode II

The entry of the subject in C minor runs its full course and establishes strongly the tonality of the *sub-dominant minor key*. After this, a passage occurs parallel to the above already described as Episode I. The chromatic descending part in the Bass of bars 3 and 4 (above) appears in the Bass, the minims remain but are placed in the Treble, and the figure x⌐▬▬▬⌐ occurs in the Alto. This section may thus be regarded as *Episode II*, being more or less the material of Episode I in changed tonality, and with two of the three parts interchanging places—an example of triple-counterpoint (freely applied).

Final Section

Analysis.—The theme now appears in the Tonic key in the Treble voice. It is slightly extended by a Codetta x⌐▬▬▬ which consists of the last germ of the Subject, repeated twice. (It will be remembered that the Codetta in the Exposition sprang from a germ of the *Counter-subject*.) It is worth showing because of the free movement of the theme:

---

[1] Professor E. J. Dent in his pamphlet 'Notes on Fugue for Beginners' in discussing the middle entries asks how this middle section 'may become more emotional, more exciting, more fantastic than the Exposition'. He says, 'We may shorten the Subject or use part of it. This applies particularly to subjects of the Handelian type with a *head* and *tail*. Sometimes the *head* alone is used, and sometimes the *tail* by itself, though the *tail generally lends itself more to treatment as material for Episodes.*'

It might be said that Frescobaldi used the *tail*, or at least the more active or later idea of the subject, in the episodes of the above fugue.

The Answer, after its first bar, develops the germ of the second bar, as in Episode I and II, in fact showing an inversion of Episode I. The Subject is taken up in the Bass, is modified and extended, a fourth voice steals in again so that the concluding eight bars are in four parts. Finally the Subject appears in the uppermost voice and runs its full course, being rounded off by an unexpected and charming cadence. This last appearance of the theme is over a tonic pedal.

To sum up

The broad outline of the fugue is:

> Exposition and Counter-exposition.
> Episode I in triple counterpoint.
> Theme in sub-dominant minor key—one entry.
> Episode II, parallel to Episode I in material and treatment, and showing an interchanged version of the triple counterpoint.
> Final Section, showing the theme and answer with freedom, and ending with Tonic Pedal.

Observations

I. Apart from the short space when the sub-dominant minor key is touched, the fugue oscillates between Tonic and Dominant minor keys.

II. There is no regular counter-subject.

III. There are examples of sequential repetition of a figure, but not of figure development.

IV. There is no example of stretto or canon.

V. The Episodes show short considerations of interchangeable counterpoint. They are also noticeable in so far as they start from the theme, which is abandoned after a bar, and proceed by sequential treatment of the figure in the second bar of the theme.

VI. There is no dominant pedal; there is a tonic pedal.

VII. The subject does not appear in a major key.

On the whole it may justly be looked upon as a fine forerunner of Bach; indeed we know that Bach diligently studied the works of Frescobaldi.

Nothing more helpful and impressive could now take place than an examination and performance of Bach's '48'. This would reveal to the earnest student what Bach has achieved and why he is so great. Gems, such as Book I, No. 2 in C minor, Book I, No. 7 in E♭ major, Book I, No. 9 in E major, Book II, No. 17 in A♭ major, show Bach's amazing flow of technique, his variety of thought, his ingenuity.

Of No. 9 in E major, Cecil Gray writes, 'To analyse this little masterpiece would be to dissect a butterfly.' Nevertheless, one may add, we should learn much by studying it in every detail.

Chapter One

THE LAY-OUT OF A FUGUE, ABSORBING THE CHIEF DEVICES USED BY BACH

This, our first consideration, is also our first essential. The lay-out must be clear in our mind, for in the examination-room there is no time to waste. If twenty students worked the same fugue subject according to the same lay-out, twenty different fugues would be the outcome; having a plan in mind just helps facility, and increases the student's power to make the most of the scope which opens up as the plan develops. A student's ability to take advantage of that scope also depends upon his skill and alertness in using his material.

Bach's bewildering variety of lay-out was governed by what the inspiration of the subject offered. But he was a master, and any student who can create a fugue with anything approaching Bach's perfection does not need this book—much less the lay-out that it commends.

The First Decision

The Exposition

Cecil Gray says of Bach's fugues '*After* the exposition, however, in which the voices enter one by one with Subject and Answer alternately according to the number of parts, almost anything may—and generally does—happen with Bach.' He had already pointed out that 'in the form as Bach practised it, only one principle is invariable—that of the exposition so-called, in which the Subject is first announced alone, and then answered by another voice, while the first voice continues with a counterpoint to it'. But even the expositions of his fugues had variety of treatment within themselves, and in the first fugue of all, the exposition is irregular! The Subject is in the alto and its Answer in the treble, being followed first by the Answer in the tenor and then by the Subject in the bass instead of vice versa. Of the first set of twenty-four:

Six have no regular counter-subject;

Eighteen expositions show regular counter-subjects in double and triple counterpoint.

Here we will make our First Decision

THE EXPOSITION TO BE WRITTEN IN DOUBLE OR TRIPLE COUNTERPOINT WITH REGULAR COUNTER-SUBJECT.

This choice is made because of the interest it will offer as the fugue proceeds.

The exposition decided upon, what to follow? Bach indulged in extra entries of the theme, or even in a varied restatement of the exposition, termed a counter-exposition; but there is no need for these things in our lay-out for an examination fugue.

The Second Decision

The First Episode

The next ground to be covered is that between the exposition and the appearance of the theme in a new key. This bridging offers scope for contrapuntal device and, of course, skill in using it (which is the real test). This bridging is usually called an Episode and its purpose is to lead from the key ending the exposition to that in which the next entry of the theme is to be made.

What contrapuntal devices can be displayed in this episode? Here are some used by Bach:

Sequential repetition of a figure or phrase.

Sequential repetition of a figure or phrase, extended by means of figure development.

Material exhibiting double or triple counterpoint.

Material showing imitation of a free kind.

Material showing canonic imitation.

Material carrying forward, in a coherent manner, an idea already heard.

Material exhibiting double or triple counterpoint with an interchange of it within the same episode.

The material used in all these cases springs from some idea in the subject, counter-subject or codetta (the link which often occurs between a subject and its answer, or answer and subject). The point to be decided is—which of the above devices shall we use in the first Episode?

Here we will make our Second Decision

THE FIRST EPISODE TO BE WRITTEN SHOWING SEQUENTIAL REPETITION EXTENDED BY MEANS OF FIGURE DEVELOPMENT WITH A PART AGAINST IT IN DOUBLE COUNTERPOINT, OR PARTS AGAINST IT IN TRIPLE COUNTERPOINT.

This choice is made because of the possibility and probability of its use in an interchanged form later. (As in *Bach*, Vol. I, No. 2.)

The Third Decision

The first middle entry or entries

The appearance of the theme in a related key now follows. The key will be other than the dominant, already used for the Answer in the Exposition. The appearance or appearances of the theme in the first related key is often called 'the first middle entry' or 'the first set of middle entries' (because probably another set is to be brought into play later).

The point to be decided is—'How many times shall the theme or the answer appear?' It is obvious that a treatment in this new key, equal to a full exposition, is not called for; balance of tonality and length of fugue have to be borne in mind. In some three-part fugues of reasonable length by Bach, one entry of the theme sufficed at this stage. Bearing in mind the necessity of keeping the complete fugue within fair working length:

Here we will make our third decision

THE FIRST MIDDLE ENTRY TO CONSIST OF A SINGLE ENTRY OF THE SUBJECT.

This choice is made because, in addition to the considerations of the length of the fugue as a whole, it postpones the introduction of stretto with advantage as will be seen.

The Fourth Decision

The Second Episode

Now follows the second episode, and the matter to be decided is—Which of the remaining devices already set out, when considering the first episode, shall be used? So far in our scheme we have employed sequential and figure development work, double- or triple-counterpoint. Our first purpose is to show as much variety of device as will fit well into our lay-out and give proof of our knowledge of contrapuntal equipment. An episode provides an excellent opportunity for canon or free imitative work.

Here we will make our fourth decision

THE SECOND EPISODE TO CONSIST OF CANONIC WORK

This choice is made because CANON affords an attractive variety of interest at this stage of the growth of the fugue.

The Fifth Decision

The Second set of Middle Entries—stretto

Appearances of the theme—the second set of middle entries—now take place in another related key or keys. The decision to be made is—How many times shall the theme or its answer appear? It must be borne in mind that as the fugue flows along it should become increasingly interesting. The effect of allowing another entry of the theme (or its answer) before the first has run its full course creates *new* interest. This device is

termed *stretto*. This $_S$————^{A}———— is normal, this $_S$————^{A}———— is stretto
Two or possibly three voices may take part as may prove convenient, but
two should suit the purpose generally.

Here we will make our fifth decision

THE SECOND MIDDLE ENTRIES TO EMPLOY STRETTO DEVICE. TWO
VOICES, POSSIBLY THREE.

The Sixth Decision

The Third Episode

Now follows the third episode. The decision concerning the material
for this was hinted at when the first episode was under consideration.
The choice of method for the first episode was because of the probability
of its use, *in an interchanged form*, later. The moment for such use has now
arrived.

Here we will make our sixth decision

THE THIRD EPISODE TO BE AN INTERCHANGED FORM OF THE FIRST EPISODE,
WITH APPROPRIATE CHANGE OF KEY.

The Seventh Decision

The Final Section

The final section of the fugue now comes under our view. Of what
shall it consist? In any case let it be our purpose to make it the culminating
period of interest, the climax of the fugue in the sense of emotion, stress
and vitality. It must be designed accordingly.

What resources may we call upon? Here are some of them:

(a) The double- or triple-counterpoint of the Exposition may be used
showing an interchange.

(b) The stretto device may be used with greater intensity than in the
second set of middle entries; that is, the entries may be at closer distances.

(c) The dominant pedal is a valuable asset, as may be the tonic pedal
finally.

(d) Free imitative entries, often called mock stretti, which might be
used against the final entry of the theme in the bass.

(e) A climax by means of figure-development, extending the theme.

(f) The subject may be altered in a manner likely to add fresh interest,
and it may be treated anew harmonically.

(g) The subject may appear in contrary motion.

(h) The subject may appear in augmentation (in notes of double their
original value) whilst against it there may be relevant figuration or contrapuntal interest.

(i) The subject may appear in diminution (in notes of half their original value). The employment of augmentation or diminution will depend upon the type of subject. A subject moving in longish notes is not likely to invite treatment by augmentation whereas a subject in short notes may do so—and so on.

The point to be decided is, 'Which of the above ideas may be appropriately used in our scheme?'

Here we will make our Seventh Decision

THE FINAL SECTION TO INCORPORATE

Possibly Double- or Triple-counterpoint of the Exposition in interchanged form.

Possibly Stretti at a shorter distance than before, though not necessarily so.

Dominant pedal (though not necessarily in three-part fugue) over which stretti would be worked.

Extension of the subject at the last stretto entry.

Free imitation, mock stretti over the final entry of the subject leading to a climax by this means.

Possibly a short coda over tonic pedal.

The points raised and the decisions made in this chapter will be *considered in detail in the following pages,* as also will *modifications of the lay-out* and an alternative shortened version. It is obvious that if a theme is given out in the tenor, the detailed behaviour of the voices affecting the 'inside' workings of the structure will be different from such behaviour had the theme been announced by the alto, although the 'inside' workings will be parallel. It is well therefore to draw maps of the skeleton fugue which will give a bird's-eye view of the lay-out—for then, before beginning actual work, the student will see just how each voice will behave, for example, when it will have the theme, what part it will play in an episode, when it will rest, and so on. Such a map would merely act as a guide, of course. Here is a rough plan of:

THE LAY-OUT OF A FUGUE

THE LAY-OUT OF THE WHOLE FUGUE

Exposition	Episode I	Middle Entry First Set	Episode II	Middle Entry Second Set	Episode III	Final Section Possibly Inverted Exposition
Involving double Counterpoint possibly triple-Counterpoint. Codetta space	Sequential with Figure development Extension double- or triple-Counterpoint	One appearance of the theme	Canonic or free imitational work	Two (or more) appearances of the theme in stretto (not too close)	An Interchanged Version of Episode I	Closer stretti over dominant pedal though not always. Extension by figure development, (possibly augmentation and diminution). Final entry with mock stretti, or free figuration work leading to climax. Possible tonic pedal coda
Tonic Major Tonic Minor		Relative Minor Relative Major		Sub-dominant major Sub-dominant minor		Tonic major Tonic minor

It is hardly necessary to remind the student that Bach would not incorporate in any particular fugue *all* possible contrapuntal devices—a glance at the first of the '48' will prove how he may concentrate on one device—in this case 'stretto'. But when Bach wrote it his mind was already the master-mind at work; he had left apprentice days behind.

THE LAY-OUT OF A FUGUE

Here is a rough plan of

AN ALTERNATIVE (and possibly SHORTER) LAY-OUT
involving two episodes only

Exposition	Episode I	Middle Entry	Episode II	Final Section
As above	Sequential and shewing interchange of its double counterpoint within its own ground. Possibly figure development and extension	The theme to appear twice, that is there should be two entries, subject and subject or subject and answer. Possibly in slight stretto. If no stretto, the codetta (if one) of the exposition may be used between the two entries (shewing an interchanged version of that codetta)	Canonic or free imitational work	As above

Tonic Major	Relative minor (or sub-dominant major)		Tonic major
Tonic Minor	Relative major (or sub-dominant minor)		Tonic minor

Chapter Two

OBSERVATIONS CONCERNING FUGUE SUBJECTS

Students, judging from their work, often give the impression that they approach every fugue subject with dread, regarding each one as some puzzling concoction designed to baffle them and bring about their doom in the examination room.

The truth is that a fugue subject is an organic structure and should be a well-built thing; if not, it is not a fair subject to work upon.[1] A good fugue subject is invested with either melodic or rhythmic power, or both; the stress may be toward one or the other, or both. A good melody is not necessarily a good subject for a fugue, though it may be excellent for a sonata; on the contrary, a good fugue subject may possess no particular melodic attractiveness.

Fugue subjects are not, as a rule, lengthy; often they are short and pithy, distinguished in one way or another; some characterized by rhythmic strength and vigour; some by boldness of line; some by tenderness, for there are also fugues which make their appeal by this noble quality.

Some subjects have sparkling vitality, some emotional depth, some foreshadow the building up of a dignified architecture in sound. Here are four of Bach's fugal themes. Play them, hum them, think them. Do they not almost tell you the kind of thing that is likely to evolve from each one?

Ex. 10

[1] Fugue subjects, *good* fugue subjects, do not necessarily call for or yield to the same treatment. Apropos of this the following incident is related by Forkel concerning Bach when he visited the King-Elector at Potsdam.

'After a time Bach asked the King to give him a subject for a Fugue, that he might treat it extempore. The King did so, and expressed his astonishment at

29

OBSERVATIONS CONCERNING FUGUE SUBJECTS

As for example:

(a) Suggests a deftly woven tapestry.

(b) Suggests a playful scherzo.

(c) Suggests an intimate contemplation.

(d) Suggests architectural grandeur.

Subjects and their construction

The previous remarks have referred to the character inherent in fugue subjects, but observations must be made bearing upon method in building them. It is impossible here to make exhaustive inquiry this into matter, but our purpose may be well served by giving attention to the four subjects already quoted.

(a) Appears to be an indivisible whole.

(b) Is possessed of an idea, figure, or germ which carries all before it.

(c) Has two parts, akin to versicle and response.

(d) Has two parts strongly contrasted—a stately opening followed by a free flowing passage.

The old Italian writers called these contrasting sections 'soggetto' and 'andamento'; they have been tersely styled 'head' and 'tail'. Many of their fugue subjects are built upon this plan, and the two divisions are distinctly separated. The above subjects are only a few of the many types of fugal themes, but they illustrate well enough things which our ears and eyes should be quick to note; things which will be of value when considering the Counter-subject and Answer.

Sequential figures in Fugue subjects

A figure may be treated sequentially in building up a fugue subject. This is an observation simple enough to make, no doubt, but it can be of immense value when the invention of the counter-subject is being undertaken, as will be shown later.

The Harmonic Foundation or Route; the rhythmic pattern of the chord-changes

It should be realized that a well-built subject must have a firm harmonic foundation; it must run on a good track of chords. The chordal changes along this track are not haphazard happenings, but generally make a rhythmic pattern or design, or tread, of their own. This is a fundamental point, to which attention must be given. The chordal changes may tread, for example, as follows:

Bach's profound skill at developing it. Anxious to see to what lengths the art could be carried, the King desired Bach to improvise a six-part fugue. But as every subject is not suitable for polyphonic treatment Bach himself chose a theme.'

Bach *knew* that the King's subject would not yield to the polyphonic scheme and would not attempt it.

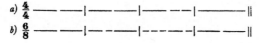

These are only imaginary, but generally speaking the start will be made in longish steps, say two in a bar and become shorter as the cadential point is approached where a long step suggests feeling of repose. *The chordal changes have rhythm*, for it would be monotonous if the same pattern were maintained bar after bar. This very error is a subtle thing—you can easily recognize melodic tautology, but harmonic tautology seems more hidden. One would think that a student would feel harmonic tautology, but my experience dictates otherwise. I have seen an exercise of some twenty bars in length with two chords in a bar kept up from beginning to end. The student said he'd always been told 'to settle the bass first' —it hadn't taken long to settle the bass and everything else with it! (The opening bar only of the exercise had been given.) The inability to see clearly the stepping-stones along the correct harmonic path is a most serious handicap to the student. It frustrates his ability (and he doesn't know *why*), it results in queer chord progressions and awkward counter-point—in a word, bad work.

The following subject may be helpful as illustrating the above matters. The *harmonic foundation* is shown by chord indications, and the *rhythmic pattern of the chordal changes* is also marked.

This shows pattern and order about the chordal tread. It begins slowly without any feeling of tension, — —|— — —|, and speeds up somewhat towards the end and climax of the subject in bar 6, — — — —|— —. This kind of thing should be carefully borne in mind; as I have already said, many students seem to be entirely unaware of it. This subject also shows *sequence* in its build-up; bars 1-2 are rhythmically reiterated in bars 3-4, and the first half of bar 5 is repeated in melodic sequence in the second half. Perhaps it would not be out of place here to complete the *counter-subject*, running along the indicated harmonic track, and illus-trating how the observance of sequence and rhythmic chordal pattern assists inventiveness and creates work of character.

The same points are illustrated by the following excerpt from Bach's '48', Vol. I, No. 15; but everything is accomplished by the great master-mind with such ease that it looks obvious; yet its subtlety is exceeded only by its grace.

This is quite a simple passage from Bach, but it serves to show how in his contrapuntal thought and practice, this great master *observed and maintained the age-long right of MELODY to pass on her way unimpeded by HARMONY even though this should cause momentary discordance*. It is quite clear that such momentary discordances are the spice of Bach's work, for without them it would be minus its essence and bite; it would resemble distilled water, pure no doubt, but tasteless.

This 'bite' is the characteristic which largely accounts for the difference between Bach's fugal work and that of the Italian school of writers which not only was contemporary with him, but which also followed him. Undoubtedly Bach was progressive—too progressive and virile for the Italians—but not iconoclastic, for he was merely extending the work of Palestrina. His work was unaffected by the new Italian style which, though mellifluous, was placid in comparison with his. For proof of this one need only play examples by Pasquini (1637-1710), Pollaroli (1650-1722), Durante (1684-1755), Domenico Scarlatti (1685-1757), Porpora (1686-1766), and Martini (1684-1756) among others. That the work of these composers had a charm no one would deny; nor would anyone deny that Cherubini (1760-1842) possessed great contrapuntal fugal skill after the Italian manner, but personally I find it impossible to regard the work of Cherubini, as seen in the Three-Part Fugue on page 76 of his *Treatise on Counterpoint and Fugue* (Novello Edition, published 1854), as at all on the same plane as the masterpieces of J. S. Bach as seen in the '48', which traverse the whole range of human feeling. The Cherubini fugue is given below. Let the student compare it with say the E major, Vol. I, No. 9, or any of the three-part fugues in the '48'.

OBSERVATIONS CONCERNING FUGUE SUBJECTS

REAL FUGUE IN THREE PARTS

Note.—This fugue, with all markings, is printed from Cherubini's book, pp. 76–9. It is preceded by the following comments:—

"This fugue, by the nature of its subject, compels the frequent employment of the chromatic genus; and by its features, and the multiplicity of its notes, it attains an instrumental character."

Digression formed of several imitations of the subject, and of the 1st counter-subject

Subject inverted

1st counter-subject inverted

Response to the subject inverted

1st counter-subject inverted

Chapter Three

THE COUNTERSUBJECT

Because the devising of a counter-subject (C.S.) is so dependent upon the important matters discussed in the previous chapter, I have chosen to consider it now and defer the problems of the Answer to a later stage.

Qualities of the C.S.

In Chapter I the First Decision states that the Exposition should be written with the C.S. in *double-counterpoint*, and possibly in triple-counterpoint. What does this mean?

It means that the C.S., like the subject itself, must be capable of proper treatment as a Bass. It must be a good workable bass conforming to the rules governing a bass part, because sooner or later it will appear in the bass.

Besides being in double-counterpoint, the C.S., as its name implies, must be in *contrast to the subject*.

Not only so, it must be *complementary to the subject*.

The two must *belong to each other*. Together they must make good, suitable *texture*.

How can these qualities be achieved?

By investing the C.S. with:

    A. Individuality of melodic line and character.
    B. Individuality of rhythmic impulse.

Let us consider these.

A. *Individuality of melodic line and character*

Point i. This does not mean that the C.S. must move in contrary motion to the subject at all costs, as though there were no virtue in similar motion. The C.S. will aim at contrary motion with the subject *generally*, without eschewing similar motion as though it were musical poison. I have often seen contrary motion pursued with dire results.

Point ii. But in aiming to obtain this individuality by contrasting the melodic line of the C.S. with that of the subject, it must be borne in mind that the C.S. must create *good two-part harmony as well as counterpoint*. This imposes restrictions (in addition to those demanded by double-counterpoint), for it is quite possible to write a well-contrasted melody which will *not* make acceptable two-part harmony. Thus for example:

Now this C.S. is not without good points, but it is unacceptable because it fails to create good two-part harmonic effect.

The following is better:

Point iii. A group of notes forming a characteristic feature of the subject should, as a rule, be avoided in composing the C.S.; in any case, such a group should be used circumspectly and with definite purpose, for it would be likely otherwise to interfere with our intention of creating contrast. For example, in the following C.S. the third bar copies the rhythm of the second bar in the subject and is too suggestive of it, particularly as it is repeated sequentially:

The above is the work of a student who was on the right track as regards certain observations, but the use of the figure (a) might well have been avoided, and some fresh idea brought into play:

Point iv. Yet in certain circumstances, such a characteristic group of notes from the subject may be used in the C.S. and help to combine the two parts, giving unity and creating good texture. But careful judgment is called for as is illustrated in the following from Bach, Vol. I, 6:

Here we see a group of four semiquavers a⌐‾‾‾⌐ used in the subject and also in the C.S. Besides exact similarity of rhythm there is a definite similarity of shape in the figure as shown in all cases where a⌐‾‾‾⌐ occurs, but the *nature* of the group as it occurs in the subject is quite different from the nature of the group as it occurs in the C.S. The significance of the group in the subject cannot be measured without including the following note B♭ taken by leap of a sixth; it is thus strong and arresting, whereas in the C.S. the groups have a placid flow. Nevertheless they form an appropriate complement to the subject and the whole makes good texture.

Therefore as a general rule:

A new figure or figures should be devised for the C.S. rather than use be made of a rhythmical idea taken from the subject.

This is shown simply enough in the following example:

Point v. Rarely are melodies (S. and C.S.) found contrasting in curve only. It is most likely, as may have been noticed already, that they contrast in rhythm also.

Even in the following where the S. and C.S. move note against note and the difference is in curve only, it might be guessed that Bach has a definite purpose in this, that he is withholding something; and this is revealed to be so later on when a new C.S. is introduced with great effect.

Let us now turn to the second type of individuality.

B. Individuality of rhythmic impulse.

Obviously this characteristic is vitally important, and there are interesting points about it to be considered.

Point i. A practical matter. It is essential to develop the power of sensing rhythmic pattern, of feeling counter rhythmic impulse as the subject is heard in our mind. With this express object in view, without giving any thought at first to melodic line, rhythmic patterns snould be plotted out, tapped out, against the subject—not one pattern but several, in fact, until possibilities seem exhausted. By this practice, rhythmic alertness, awareness, inventiveness may be developed. The idea will be grasped if the rhythm of the C.S. against the following subject is made a matter of experiment.

The subject should be written out (not merely its rhythm) and all counter-subjects devised upon proper harmonic progression and observance of sequence. The experiment begins with the simplest rhythm; each succeeding effort should increase in rhythmic interest. The final choice may depend upon the tempo of the subject; the whole must have coherency and balance not only with reference to the subject, but also within itself. Such experimenting is worth while; it will do much to increase discrimination and judgment as to what is acceptable material.

Besides the above general suggestions regarding rhythm, there are others concerning shape, construction and purpose which may assist in the final decision on the C.S. These spring from the careful study of the make-up of the subject.

Point ii. Long notes versus short notes.

When the S. is indulging in long notes the C.S. will be on the look-out for what can be done by short notes. This is clearly the case in the following:

Point iii. Sequential work, melodic and rhythmic.

When the S. contains ideas treated sequentially, the C.S. is likely to introduce parallel sequential treatment (though not of necessity). This

41

is shown in the following where both the rhythm and melodic contour are repeated.

There is slight modification of bar 2 of the C.S. in bar 3, from which may be gathered the fact that Bach was quite aware that there is no virtue in mere exactness, which would mean a repetition of the first half of bar 2 at the first half of bar 3. Such exactness would have somewhat hindered the increasing drive of the C.S. towards its climax. Bach applied the spirit of the idea of sequence, not the letter.

N.B.—Thus, instead of a C.S. which merely bustles about, is created one which bustles about intelligently, having musical value and purpose. See to it in any case, sequential or otherwise, that you *think* your C.S. in flights; this will prevent aimless movement, such as is incapable of being phrased, and devoid of repose points.

Point iv. Sequential work, rhythmic only.

Sequential work may include repetition of the rhythm of a pattern, without preserving the contour of the melody. This type of thing is valuable. It is shown in the following where the rhythmic repetition in the subject is balanced by rhythmic repetition in the C.S., but without any intention of preserving any melodic contour in the sequence.

Point v. Further sequential examples.

A subject incorporating sequential treatment, may have a C.S. which does not indulge in parallel sequence at all. Thus:

On the other hand, a subject not containing sequence may have a C.S. which does, as is shown in the following:

THE COUNTERSUBJECT

It would be worth the student's while to try to discover why Bach acted as he did in such cases.

To sum up regarding sequential work (for examination fugues).

It would be advisable to balance any sequential play in the subject by parallel sequential play in the C.S.

This is excellently displayed in the following:

This example further illustrates the point discussed on page 39, Point iv —the use of a figure from the subject, in the C.S. And in this instance the figure ⌣ₓ⌣ from the S. appears exactly in the same form and shape at ⌣ₓ⌣ in the C.S. But the point to bear in mind is, that this figure is not the *basis* of the C.S., it is used at the end against the long trilled note and undoubtedly justifies its use, for it makes a most appropriate texture.

Point vi. Persistency of a figure in the C.S

The C.S. under Point v illustrates in some measure another important matter, namely—the persistency of a figure in the C.S.

The idea of a figure persisting, and possibly developing, may help in giving the C.S. purpose, drive, unity, and indeed an individuality. This is seen in the above at ⌐ₐ⌐, ⌐_b⌐, ⌐ₐ⌐ in the C.S.

In the following example the figure ♫♫ persists and drives onward to a climax—it carries all before it:

In the next example a similar persistency occurs plus development, and thus the passage gathers momentum:

Point vii. Overcrowding the texture.

But it must be borne in mind that it is possible to crowd too much into the texture of the S. and C.S.

There is danger, too, lest, where the third and later voices enter with the theme, no room be left for the two opening voices to enter into the conversation or contribute their fair share of interest as counter-subjects or free parts.

It will be noticed that the semiquaver work at the beginning of the C.S. stops abruptly and gives way to crochets. The reason is apparent enough, for it thus affords the original subject-voice fair opportunity to converse and contribute something worth while when the third voice makes its appearance at X, thus creating good texture besides distributing the interest.

Another and valuable illustration of this same point is to be seen in Bach, Vol. II, 10. The student will be wise to examine this. He should also explore for himself and make his own further discoveries concerning counter-subjects, because the observations made in this chapter make no pretence at being exhaustive. All the counter-subjects used in this chapter are intended to be regular—that is, for use, if desired, with the subject whenever it appears—and are therefore written in double counterpoint.

Point viii. A further word regarding the material of the C.S.

It is obvious that all which this chapter presents, must, in practice, have important influence upon the unfolding of the fugue, because it must bring into being material which is vital (has life), material which has character, and which may and probably will be called upon for further service in the episodes.

Some idea from the C.S. may be the inspiring force of an episode. Note the word inspiring; some idea from the C.S. should be *capable* of being the inspiration of an episode—that is the meaning the word should convey.

Inspiration does away with concoction, and too often have I seen episodes which were mere concoctions.

So we may say that Episodes will not be matters of chance or good luck; for we can see to it that they shall belong both to what precedes and what follows them and thus help to give the fugue organic unity.

Chapter Four

THE CODETTA—ITS IMPORTANCE AND POTENTIALITY

What a codetta is and where it occurs

Case I

When a fugue subject (S.) has been announced, a second voice is due to enter with a response or answer (A.) which is a new statement of the subject at a different level or pitch, usually at the fifth above in the dominant key. There are occasions when the ending of the S. is not a convenient moment for the A. to enter.

Case II

Similarly, and perhaps more often, when the A. has been completed the moment may not be convenient for the immediate re-entry of the S. in a third voice. In both these cases the S. or A. must be prolonged until an appropriate moment for the entry of the next voice is reached.

The material between the end of the S. or A. and the next entry of the theme is called a CODETTA.

The material is important because of its possible and probable use at a later stage as the basis of an episode.

This codetta space therefore must not be occupied by mere padding exhibiting poverty of thought and invention. The manner in which this space is treated creates an impression, favourable or otherwise, on the examiner.

The material of the codetta

The following are three of Bach's ways of using the codetta space:

(a) The codetta material may spring from the ending of the subject and appear to be a continuation of it.

(b) The codetta material may arise out of an idea occurring earlier in the subject.

(c) The codetta material may be new, but having affinity with the S.; or being in contrast with it, yet in some sense responsive or complementary to it, may appear as a continuation of the subject as in (a).

Let us examine illustrations of these three treatments, in both Case I and Case II.

46

THE CODETTA

Illustrations in Case I

Note.—As a rule the codetta space here (between S. and A.) will be short and will not therefore necessitate any serious or prolonged drawing-out of the chosen idea or germ.

(a) In this example the ending of the subject is extended, making the completed bar 6 a sequential repetition of the penultimate bar 5, the chosen idea a⌐▬▬⌐ being tacked on to the subject which ends at *. The codetta appears to be a continuation of the subject.

(b) Examples of the codetta springing from an idea in the earlier or middle part of the subject are not numerous. There would seem to be more opportunity for such a procedure in Case II when the codetta links up the Answer to the next entry of the subject. In any case, however, there is danger in picking out an idea from the middle of the theme, for it may not fit on to the end at all naturally. It needs careful judgment. It is more likely that a mere suggestion for the codetta may occur during the course of the subject. Such would seem to be so in the following instance.

The germ a⌐▬▬▬⌐ in the subject does seem to be a suggestive idea for the codetta which begins with it and then runs along scale-wise and creates a new thing.

(c) New material, having affinity with the subject, or being in some sense responsive or complementary to it, even if in contrast with it, seems to be quite frequently called into play.

Bach's examples all seem to be inevitable and hide the skill that made them so.

(i) The following is a good example of the codetta a⌐▬▬▬⌐, showing strong affinity with the subject by means of its rhythm which coincides with the opening half-bar of the subject.

(ii) The following is a case in which the codetta—new material—gathers its urge and sweep from the final bar of the Subject where the impetus begins. The result is an effect of continuous subject-matter overlapping the Answer, driving into the Counter-subject.

Besides the onward sweep, note that the cadence point at * (the end of the S.) is passed over and is merely a momentary realization.

(iii) This next example resembles the above (ii) in impetus and sweep, but the line or curve of the ending of the subject is not maintained. The semiquaver movement surges onwards, but with change of direction at y; this contrast leads to an interesting recurrence of the figure x⌐▬▬⌐ which ends the subject.

It is an example that will repay careful consideration.

The actual connecting link (the rising figure y) plays no part beyond the Exposition, nor is it sufficiently striking to do so. Bach chooses other ideas for Episodes. It just joins the end of the subject a⌐▬▬⌐ to the C.S., which begins also with the figure x⌐▬▬⌐. It is interesting that this figure fits the first two beats of the subject.

It will be readily conceded that the invention of a short codetta is not as easy to achieve as these appear to be. They seem inevitable, unalterable; but, leave the codetta space blank, and attempt to supply the material yourself!

There are cases when the end of the subject creates a decided point of repose, from which the codetta has, as it were, to start up again.

The following is such a case, and the student should attempt to fill the codetta space—and possibly a little beyond—in several ways.

THE CODETTA

It should be noted at the outset, the figure a⌐▬▬ appears three times in the subject, so that any use of it in the codetta is unlikely.

It is worth while to look carefully beyond the Exposition to see what material Bach uses in his episodes and whence it comes. For example, in the Organ Fugue in G minor above, it is evident that he was more attracted by ideas within the S. and C.S. than by the codetta, for he made no further use of the latter. Not that it was inappropriate for the particular purpose for which it was fitted. But it provides evidence that not always is the codetta intended for more than a small local rôle. It would seem that the larger codetta space in Case II offers more opportunity than the shorter space in Case I.

Illustrations in Case II

(a). The following shows the codetta as a perfect continuation or expansion of the S., the last idea of which is repeated in sequence, twice. This method was much favoured by Bach. (See also Vol. I, 2.)

(b). The following codetta draws its idea from the middle of the subject, just four notes in upward step-wise succession. Reference has already been made to the danger of choosing an idea from the middle of a theme, lest its rhythm should isolate it or make it difficult to dovetail on to the end of the subject. Care should be taken in the choosing of such an idea, that it should be the beginning of a flight and coincide with a phrase- point. This, as we should expect, is observed by Bach in the following instances:

The codetta is created by an imitative treatment of x , which prolongs the subject as it were, in a relevant and interesting manner.

Obviously x▬▬ coincides with a phrase-point and fits perfectly on to the end of the subject. The codetta is made by the sequential repetition of x which is responded to in contrary motion by the other voice.

(c). (i). The following shows a codetta built upon a new idea, but in keeping with the character of the subject material.

The part of the codetta marked x has rhythmic affinity with the opening of the subject. Again Bach indulges in free canonic conversation between the voices and thus builds up the codetta.

(ii). It is difficult to refrain from quoting the following, in which a codetta between A. and S. is built up on a new idea, in keeping with, and yet in contrast to, the S. and C.S.; besides which it shows Bach's fecundity of ideas in that the material is treated in contrary motion and in different voices in successive bars. It will be noticed that x▬▬ has rhythmic affinity with the opening bars of the C.S.

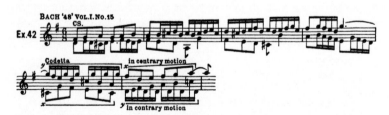

Besides these three treatments (a), (b), (c), which apply in both Case I and Case II, Bach sometimes called upon the resources of the Counter-subject which of course could only be used in Case II—that is, for the codetta linking the Answer to the next entry of the subject.

This is shown in the following:

The codetta in bar 5 is a modification tonally of the C.S. in bar 3. Thus the first bar in the C.S. is drawn upon—not in part, but fully—to form the codetta.

Even from these few observations and examples it will be seen that the codetta is important and has possibilities; possibilities as a valuable factor in the unfolding scheme of the fugue. Therefore the codetta deserves careful thought and must have it. The fact is, it is one of those little places in which our musicianship is thoroughly searched out.

Chapter Five

THE ANSWER

An historical approach

The relations between Subject and Answer have long been beset by what the late Sir Donald Tovey called 'vexatious minutiae'. These difficulties have become all the more puzzling because—according to almost all theorists—even the ways of our great authority J. S. Bach are at times past understanding, and appear to be inexplicable. But what help is it if we refer to Bach as our authority and yet are unable to explain and elucidate what he does?

In this chapter we shall seek illumination by way of historical approach to the problems of subject and answer. We shall examine customs and freedoms of earlier days; we shall see if such customs and freedoms were recognized, practised and applied by such great masters as Purcell and Bach. We shall see if, by examining Bach's methods in the light of these customs, we are able to elucidate and explain at least some of the difficulties that authors in the past have failed to solve.

It may be stated here and now that we shall find, clearly established for us, a direct line of continuity from those earlier days away on through Purcell to Bach. And, it is hoped, by the study of this way of approach, we may see more clearly how the mind of Bach worked, for then will his so-called irregularities melt away.

. . . . . .

By the term ANSWER in fugue is meant a response to the subject by another voice at a different level of pitch.

Although the Answer came to be generally regarded as being a fifth higher (or fourth lower) yet this was by no means a necessary thing in the earlier days of writing in this style. It is well to bear this in mind when trying to understand certain procedures in regard to the Answer which will be considered later.

The Exposition

If a fugue be written for three voices, the first announces the Subject, the second gives the response, the Answer, which is normally a fifth higher (and in the dominant key in our day), and the third voice enters with the Subject in the Tonic key again. All three voices having entered, the material of the fugue is 'exposed' as it were, and this section is termed the Exposition.

But as simple as this procedure appears in theory, yet in practice it is true to say that the Answer is a source of worry and confusion to the student.

Why is this?

It is because, under certain circumstances, the Answer is not a straightforward, exact transposition of the Subject. Alteration is made for some reason. The reason, at times, seems a matter of doubt, and the student becomes ill at ease, for he is not sure in his own mind whether he has effected the alteration correctly or not.

Answers, real and tonal

When the answer is an exact copy of the subject at the level of a fifth above it is termed Real.

When the answer is not an exact copy of the subject—even if only one note is not at the level of a fifth above—it is termed Tonal.

And so a fugue is termed Real or Tonal according to whether it necessitates a Real or a Tonal answer.

For the sake of convenience let us consider subjects under the headings of Real or Tonal as follows:

CLASS I. *Real* subjects which have not the dominant note at or near the beginning, and end in the Tonic key. They are answered a fifth higher in the dominant key.

CLASS II. *Tonal* subjects which modulate to and end in the dominant key. They need modification in the Answer from the point where modulation begins.

CLASS III. *Tonal* subjects which use the dominant note *at* the beginning. They usually need modification in the *immediate* Answer where this note occurs. (Procedure in later Answers is discussed under this heading.)

CLASS IV. *Tonal* subjects which use the dominant note *near* their beginning. They usually need modification in the *immediate* Answer where this note occurs. (Procedure in later Answers is discussed under this heading.)

Consideration of CLASS I

This is a matter of brevity, for the Answer is merely an exact copy of the Subject in the dominant key. This class of Subject usually begins on the Tonic note.

The following are examples:

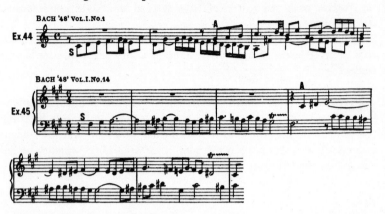

In the latter example the subject modulates but returns to the Tonic key and the Answer follows a similar path.

Consideration of CLASS II

Subjects which modulate to and end in the dominant key.

Thus, suppose a subject begins in C major and ends in G major. Were this to be responded to by an answer a fifth above, the result would be something beginning in G major and ending in D major. As the next entry would be in the tonic key C major, there would be a somewhat violent twist in tonality from D major.

The student appreciates that this is awkward musically and agrees that adjustment is necessary. He accepts it, and probably never goes more deeply into the matter.

The purpose of the adjustment is to bring the Answer to an end in C major (the original Tonic key). It may be shown thus:

> Subject begins in C, ends in G.
> Answer begins in G, ends in C.

Probably it is this necessary adjustment of tonality which gives the name Tonal to such subjects and their answers.

It all simmers down to the apparently simple idea that:

> Whatever appears in the dominant key in the subject must appear in the tonic key in the answer.

But the crux of the matter, practically, is to determine the most suitable point during the progress of the Answer from which to veer towards the Tonic key, and this is not always a simple matter.

Examination of the following examples may prove useful.

A. When the subject is of the 'head and tail' kind and the division is clear-cut, it is possible that the key change may be coincident with this division. Thus:

Another way of regarding this is:

Whatever is in the tonic is answered dominantly (a fifth above).

Whatever is in the dominant is answered sub-dominantly (a fourth above).

Of course each note in one key is answered by the corresponding degree in the other.

B. The following subject of the 'head and tail' kind reveals the fact that the dividing line between head and tail is not necessarily a help in constructing the answer, because the point of adjustment does not coincide with the dividing line.

The head and tail are marked a⬛━━━┐ and b⬛━━━┐ respectively. But close examination will show that this division into parts is no help as regards plotting the answer. In other words, we cannot apply the method which worked in the case of Bach's fugue in E flat (Ex. 46) and make the change at the joint of the head and tail as indicated at x——y in the following first sketch for the answer:

The reason is that no harmonic progression can bridge the gap between x——y satisfactorily. And it can be taken as a sure decision that any adjustment which causes forced harmonic progression, is wrongly made.

It is therefore obvious that the adjustment in the answer does not coincide with the beginning of the tail of the subject.

What then can help us to make sure of the proper adjustment? My reply is 'CADENCE-FEELING'; and cadence-feeling is supremely important.

A point about Modulation

The advice is frequently given that modulation should be looked for as early as possible in the theme; in other words it should be recognized and effected without delay. This is sound advice up to a point, and the point is being sure where modulation really takes place. It is advice which needs care in application, as will be shown.

CADENCE FEELING

Now a cadence is a falling of some kind, and in music the falling must be from a weak beat to a strong one. This is a simple fact that can be of great help, though often ignored or forgotten.

In the example under consideration:

it is clear that there is cadential feeling between the last quaver in bar 2 and the first in bar 3; and this is a cadence, a perfect or inverted perfect cadence in A minor the Tonic key, as shown by c⌐——⌐. There is no harmonic repose at the end of section a⌐——⌐ (the head); it can only be found at c. (We shall see that in bar 2 the dominant chord cannot well occur until the 3rd beat; it does not coincide with the melodic repose on the 2nd beat.) Therefore the Tonic key extends up to and includes the first quaver A in bar 3, and it follows that the same section of the Answer will appear in the Dominant key E minor. Thus:

Answer.

Therefore the adjustment must be made *after* this point, and it is clear that the 'head and tail' division does not coincide with the cadential one.

And now for the remainder of the Answer

It is an easy matter to answer the notes (in the subject) which are definitely in the Dominant key by corresponding notes (degrees) in the Tonic key. For certain the last five quavers of the subject are in the Dominant key of E minor and will be answered in A minor. Thus:

There is now only one quaver left to consider, the 2nd quaver in bar 3 of the subject marked b▭▬▭ Ex. 49.

The point arises as to how this note shall be regarded—is it in the Dominant key or the Tonic?

(x) If it is regarded as the keynote of the Dominant key in E minor, it will be answered by the keynote of the Tonic key A minor. Thus:

The phrase corresponds with the original subject and the characteristic drop of a seventh is preserved, but the gap g▭▬▭ at the joint is a fourth, whereas in the subject it is a fifth.

(y) If it is regarded as the 5th of the Tonic chord in A minor, it will be answered by the 5th of the Tonic chord in E minor (the dominant key). Thus:

The gap g▭▬▭ is a fifth as in the subject, but the characteristic drop of a seventh is lost and this complete phrase does not quite respond to the original.

Obviously it would seem better musically to make the adjustment at the joint (between the bones so to speak) of the two sections as in Ex. 52, rather than later as in Ex. 53.

The harmonic aspect

Both x and y are melodic decisions. Let us go further and consider the situation from a harmonic point of view, for a melodic outline must be capable of chordal support based on good harmonic progression. As a help I have suggested a possible counter-subject.

In this case the modulation to A minor is effected with clearness. Bar 6 begins with E minor chord; the 2nd quaver has the Tonic chord of A minor, and this is followed on the 2nd crochet beat with II 7 (B.D.F♮.A), and this is followed by V 7 on the 3rd crochet, and the passage ends with a perfect cadence in A minor.

Here the return to A minor is not satisfactorily effected. Bar 6 begins with E minor chord maintained throughout the first crochet beat; to follow this, as we must, by II 7 (B.D.F♮.A) in A minor is, to say the least of it, not usual. In fact, it is unsatisfactory.

Therefore from the harmonic aspect also, the x treatment supports the decision made melodically, of regarding the 2nd quaver in bar 3 as the Tonic of the new (dominant) key and not the fifth note of the chord of A minor (tonic key). And we can feel safe in regarding this decision as final.

So far we have discussed a subject of the 'head and tail' type, the sectional division of which is strong, but which does not coincide with the cadence-feeling and does not indicate the point of adjustment in the Tonal Answer. And we have seen that cadence-feeling is the essential element in deciding the point of modulation.

C. But let us consider another example, somewhat similar to the above subject at B, but the whole being an unbroken flow. (It was written by Sir Stanley Marchant.)

Let us remind ourselves that we are considering subjects which modulate to the Dominant key, and that we are endeavouring to determine the most suitable point from which the modulation might be considered to start—or, in other words, where the Tonic key is left behind; because upon this depends the corresponding change of key in the Answer and the point of adjustment.

Note the letters m, n, o.

Now according to where it is considered that the Tonic key is left behind, i.e. from m, n, or o, so will the Answer vary, and the three following answers must come to pass:

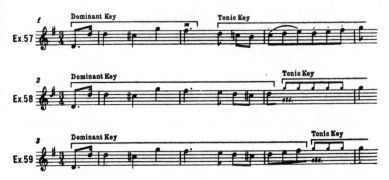

Let us consider these

Version 1. The longish note at m in the subject does coincide with a cadential feeling and it would appear that this might mark the dividing line or modulation joint we desire to find. But if so, the rest of the theme will appear in the Tonic key—in the Answer—as shown. The Subject itself must therefore be harmonized on the following basis, which is: that from m the subject leaves the Tonic key, and the rest must be harmonized in the Dominant key.

balanced in the Answer by:

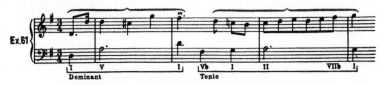

But there is something subtly unsatisfactory in bars 2 and 3 of the Answer. The swing from D major chord to A minor chord on these strong first beats is rather queer.

Suppose the subject were:

the answer surely would not be:

Ex.63

but:

Ex.64

It may be brought forward that the harmonized version given above illustrates the principle of establishing the modulation as soon as possible (see p. 56), getting into the Dominant key without delay, particularly as there is a sense of repose in the Tonic on the longish note at m. Let us examine this more closely. Attention has already been drawn to a simple fact which is often overlooked—the fact that a defining cadence is formed by Dominant to Tonic moving from a weak to a strong beat. Does this harmonization agree with this? Bar 3 shows that it does not, for the move from dominant to tonic is from a weak to a weaker beat, and there is no sense of cadence. This explains the queerness mentioned above. This treatment therefore cannot be correct; and it shows there is a danger in trying to modulate 'as early as you can'.

Turn again now to:

Version 2. This shows the Tonic key, carried by the flight of the phrase throughout the 2nd bar to the beginning of the 3rd.

It is essential that a true cadence be made, though not necessarily a perfect cadence.

Ex.65

answered thus:

Ex.66

This version, so far, appears correct.

Version 3. Can the flight of the phrase in Version 2 be extended to include the first three quavers in bar 3? That is, can we regard the Tonic key as continuing up to o? If so, the Answer would be as follows, and the basic harmony as shown:

This would leave only the last four notes ♪♪♪ |♩ of the subject for the dominant key, answered as above in the Tonic key. This seems acceptable; there is no tautological effect in bar 3 as the accent within the bar proves. The whole passage also runs smoothly—often an important point.

But let us glance again at Version 2 and complete the Answer as being in the Tonic key from n. Thus:

This version too can be justified, and some may prefer it to Version 3. A criticism against it is that the repeated note rather spoils the flow—causing a break at that point. But both versions can be proved correct, and the final choice is a matter of individual preference. Let us reason this out carefully. It would seem to depend upon what one regards as constituting a motive or figure in music—and again, it may be said that some motives are more clearly defined than others.

For example, suppose the present subject made a decided repose effect at n by means of a crotchet beat, this would clearly define the motive and phrase, and rule out any idea of continuing the Tonic key further. It would be correct to treat all the remaining notes in the Dominant. Thus:

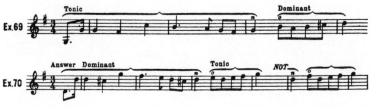

It is clear that the musical idea, the motive, completes itself at n. It is said that a motive consists of a strong beat preceded by one or more weaker beats, and if the strong beat is an appoggiatura or discord the motive includes the note of resolution. Version 2 strictly accords with this, the motive ending precisely at the strong beat (crotchet) on the first quaver.

The above definition of a motive mentions that if the strong beat is an appoggiatura, the motive includes the note of resolution. In other words the idea must complete itself, which cannot be done without including the note of resolution.

Thus one may regard a motive as extending up to the completion of an idea. Surely this may apply to an idea incomplete at the strong first beat of a bar, but not involving an appoggiatura or a discord.

The breaking-point of a wave on the shore may be regarded as the strong beat, but the wave has not spent itself—it rolls on, weakening of course. Similarly, a motive may reach its climax at the strong beat—it may end there, but also, like the wave, it may spend itself in continuing for a note or two. Version 3 accords with this idea, ending on the 3rd quaver in bar 3. This extends the Tonic key up to o which justifies the answer given.

Example from Bach parallel to Version 2:

Here the Answer corresponds to Version 2, in which the final motive ends on the strong beat. The Answer might have responded to the Subject beyond this strong beat up to o, which would however have been regarding the motive as continuing to that point.

Example from Bach parallel to Version 3, from Three-part Inventions, No. 3.

Here Bach obviously regards the motive as carrying on to o in the Tonic, and this is shown in the Answer. The notes after o in the Subject are in the Dominant key and are balanced by appearing in the Tonic key at the end of the Answer.

This detailed discussion of a small but crucial point has been purposely carried out in order to help the student to think matters out for himself on right lines. Everyone knows that such a point can cause no end of trouble, and that indecision wastes valuable time in the examination room.

Consideration of CLASS III

Subjects which use the dominant note at the beginning. (For consideration of Bach's treatment, see page 77 *et seq.*)

Let us quote from Prout's Fugue, page 32:

'The old rule for fugal answer was that a subject made in either half of the authentic scale should be answered in the corresponding half of the plagal scale, and vice-versa. For instance, if the subject began with a leap between tonic and dominant in the lower half of the authentic scale

the Answer would begin with a leap between dominant and tonic

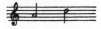

and conversely, if the subject began in the lower half of the plagal scale with a leap between dominant and tonic

the Answer would begin in the lower half of the authentic scale with the leap up from tonic to dominant.'

Roughly speaking, the ecclesiastical modes, of which there were eight in common use, went in four pairs. The two modes of each pair were closely related, for they consisted of two arrangements of the same notes and were known as authentic and plagal. Thus the Dorian Mode (Mode I) had a range from D to D, and its dominant note was A. Its related mode, the Hypo-Dorian Mode—also known as Mode II, had the same final D (what we should term tonic or doh), but its range was from A to A.

Dorian Mode (Mode I)—Authentic Range:

63

THE ANSWER

Hypo-Dorian Mode (Mode II)—Plagal Range:

Ex. 74

A melody in either the authentic or plagal range of the Mode, ended on the same note D, called the Final. The dominant note in Mode I was a fifth above the starting note D; but it will be noted that in Mode II the dominant note was not a fifth above the starting note. This is merely mentioned in passing, but this matter of the dominant note will be referred to more fully later, for it is important.

In the translation of music—dare one say during the canalization of music?—from the modes to our keys, the art of musical thinking was changed—had to change, and although modal thought, modal tonality, was gradually left behind, yet the modal habits of thinking and working lingered on, in fact, were much alive, and had influence on the habits of thinking and working in our major and minor scales. The practices of working—that is technique—in those earlier days were the foundation of our later practices. The reasons behind the customs of those modal writers, however, were lost sight of—perhaps brushed aside unheedingly by some—perhaps not known and therefore not valued or understood by others.

It is nevertheless essential for us to approach this branch of our study historically, if we are to appreciate its application as seen in the work of Bach, whom we regard as our great master of fugue.

Continuing from the statement of the old rule already quoted, we might sum up the matter by the following general statement:

The Tonic note is answered by the Dominant (fifth above).
The Dominant note is answered by the Tonic (fourth above).

I would prefer to say:

The Tonic note is answered dominantly (fifth above).
The Dominant note is answered sub-dominantly (fourth above).

In modern work we may say that a subject beginning with the Tonic note is answered dominantly always, for this note is the Tonic of the new key in which the Answer appears.

Therefore any adjustment is confined to considerations concerning the Dominant note. This note may begin the Subject, or occur near the beginning. It is the occurrence of this dominant note in the different contexts at the beginning of the subject that is the source of trouble to the student.

Why should there ever have been a rule which should bring into play considerations of the possibility of part of a scale as from D to A being answered by another part smaller in range—from A to D—he asks?

For in scalic-fugue (that is fugue founded on modern scale tonality) when the dominant note occurs at the beginning, it would seem the obvious thing to answer it by corresponding dominant note in the key of the Answer. Where did this old rule spring from? Why did it ever come into being?

(The student may be reminded that we are now considering the dominant note at the beginning of a subject—we are not considering a subject, the latter part of which has modulated to the dominant key; that has already been dealt with.)

To give the student some idea how greatly this matter has loomed before the eyes of all who have endeavoured to write about fugue, or (what is far more important) teach its technique, I would ask his forbearance as I make relevant quotations from various authors of eminence.

The late Sir Donald Tovey (from *Musical Textures*—Oxford University Press):

(a) 'The question at once arises whether the alternation between subject and answer is an alternation between *two keys* or an alternation between *two positions of the same scale.*'

(b) 'The rules governing the details of tonal answers are *vexatious*—there are numerous cases where *it is said* to be difficult to find a correct answer. The recent very learned treatise on *La Fugue d'École* by Gédalge makes out an excellent and honest case for the admittedly fictitious scholastic fugue as a discipline, but in my opinion demolishes its case completely by gravely demonstrating that for a certain subject beginning with three adjacent notes, the only correct answer is one of three identical notes, whether the fugue be scholastic or genuinely musical. *The rules which make such a case difficult ought to be swept into limbo.*'

(c) 'The rhetorical common sense of the rules that produce tonal answers becomes self-evident when we take typical instances. There are two main cross-sections of the scale, in one of which the tonic is the melodic centre and in the other the dominant. *Where either note is prominent it is answered by the other*, and where in one position the melody has a fifth in which to move, it will have only a fourth in the other position. The relation between these positions is described in terms of the ecclesiastical modes, as the relation between the authentic and plagal; but as a matter of history the tonal fugue did not take shape until the seventeenth century.'

The book by Gédalge, *La Fugue d'École*, already commented upon as above by Sir Donald Tovey, is referred to in a very different tone by the

Professor of Music at Cambridge University (1941), Dr. E. J. Dent. In his privately printed pamphlet, *Notes on Fugue for Beginners*, he refers to it as:

(d) 'the best text-book of Fugue. .... The most useful type of fugue for Academic practice is that suggested by Gédalge, *based upon the rules of Cherubini*, and accepted as the standard form by the Paris Conservatoire.'

Dr. Dent also states:

(e) 'It is noticeable that even comparatively modern composers, such as Liszt and Saint-Saëns, tend to drop into the Bach style as soon as they write fugues. It is really the Frescobaldi style, and it certainly dominates orthodox fugue for two centuries, so that even now it is singularly difficult to break away from it. That is the certain duty of the modern composer. . . .'

It is evident that these are diametrically opposed estimates of the book by Gédalge, and the comparative worth of Cherubinian and Bachian ideas —in other words, the Italian School and the Bach School. Students should read both Tovey's *Musical Textures* and Dent's *Notes on Fugues for Beginners*.

(f) Dr. Dent further states:

'Since J. S. Bach generally preferred *tonal* answers, modern teachers are inclinded to regard a tonal answer as indispensable, except in particular cases defined by rule. But Prout points out that Handel shows a great partiality for *real* answers, and Handel's authority is surely as good as anyone else's.'

It may be pointed out that of Bach's '48' there are twenty-seven tonal answers and twenty-one real answers, so this reveals no decided preference on Bach's part. I hope there is no need to challenge the authority of Bach against that of Handel; such preferences as they appear to have, in the view of Dr. Dent and Dr. Prout, may be due perhaps to greater or less adherence to, or interest in, tradition and the customs of earlier times. What these customs were will be shown later.

(g) Dr. Prout goes on:

'We now have to consider an important class of subjects—those that commence on the dominant.

'The *Old rule* again was here *absolute*—that when the subject began on the dominant the answer must begin on the tonic.'

A footnote adds, 'If, however, the dominant was an unaccented note of small value, a *real* answer was *sometimes* allowed by the old theorists,'

(h) 'We have given quite enough examples to prove that the rule as to answering dominant by tonic at the commencement of a subject is by no means so "*absolute*" as it is declared to be by some theorists.'

(j) 'The melodic form of the subject should be kept unchanged as far as possible and it is quite evident that in many cases the great composers felt this to be of much more importance than the keeping of an *old rule* that was made before modern tonality was established.'

(k) 'A further proof that but little weight was attached to the necessity for a tonal answer is found in the fact that *sometimes* in the first exposition of a fugue the first answer will be tonal and the second real as in the following case—Bach's Organ fugue in A major.'

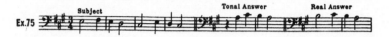

These statements from Prout spell indefiniteness and uncertainty, and are distinctly unhelpful to the student; it would seem as if two opinions were contending, the one to prove that tonal answers were right and real answers wrong and the other to prove the reverse. Be that as it may, it is evident that much clarification is required.

(l) Dr. R. O. Morris (from *The Structure of Music*, Oxford University Press), p. 93:

'The whole process (tonal and real answers) is really based on the old distinction between the 'plagal' and 'authentic' forms of the scale, and the *object of the modification* is not primarily to reproduce the subject in the dominant key (which would not of itself entail any modification), but to give its *approximate equivalent* in the corresponding plagal or authentic register.'

(m) Further Dr. Morris observes:

'Sometimes the change (of key) is deferred until nearly the end of the answer as in Bach, Vol. I, 8.'

Here we see that the tonality of the tonic key E♮ minor is maintained well into the answer. This kind of thing will be referred to later on.

(n) And Dr. Morris also writes (after making valuable explanations concerning rules for tonal answers):

'There are many modulating subjects which cannot be answered in accordance with the above rules without undue distortion. In such cases it is best to take the bull by the horns and give a *real answer starting in the sub-dominant* as Bach does in Vol. I, 18.'

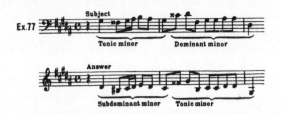

The Answer however does not *start* with a sub-dominant response; the first note D♯ is the *dominant* and expected response. This is important to observe; the Tonic degree in G♯ minor is answered by Tonic degree in D♯ minor; it is after that point that sub-dominant response begins.

(o) Sir Edward Bairstow (*Counterpoint and Harmony*, Macmillan and Stainer and Bell) stresses the same point as Dr. Morris, regarding response in the sub-dominant key. He says:

> 'Occasionally, to avoid ugliness, it is necessary to regard the Tonic as the sub-dominant of the dominant.'

But I venture to suggest that there may be some deeper explanation of the use of the sub-dominant response.

. . . .

Now, many other quotations could be added to these already given, but these must suffice to show the state of affairs and how much these tonal problems have engaged the attention of writers and teachers.

Let us summarize the points of the quoted statements.

Summary

(i). The recognition of two cross-sections of a scale is evident—doh to soh, and soh to doh, of which sections doh is the melodic centre of the former, and soh of the latter.

Further, when either note is prominent, it is answered by the other. Where in one position the melody has a fifth in which to move, it will only have a fourth in the other.

(ii). The treatise by Gédalge based upon the rules of Cherubini, is recommended by one authority and exploded by another.

(iii). There would appear to be a strife of ideas concerning the Answer, as though there were some apology needed to justify the use of a tonal answer on the one hand and a real answer on the other. Old rules (revered at one time, discarded at another) are called upon to support or decry as may suit the occasion.

(iv). There is an observation that Bach uses first a Tonal answer to a subject and later a real answer to it; and this is used as evidence that little weight was attached to the necessity of a tonal answer at all. Prout was unable to discover any more serious reason for Bach's apparently whimsical behaviour.

We shall see how essential it is to examine the full exposition of a fugue to appreciate (not only to observe) these variations between Real and Tonal Answers. Maintenance of the original tonality beyond the subject was an old custom of which Bach was aware and which he fully valued, and particularly so in cases of subjects of somewhat short length.

(v). The employment of a sub-dominant answer is regarded as a thing of rare occurrence, demanding special justification for its appearance. We shall see when Bach used it he was following one of the most common customs of earlier days.

(vi). The suggestion that 'Handel's authority was as good as anyone else's' seems quite unnecessary, because we shall see that according to earlier customs there was great liberty in respect of a subject or a note being responded to either dominantly or sub-dominantly. Handel's procedure in 'And He shall purify' (page 82) entirely agrees with the thought of Bach.

(vii). Sometimes, it is observed, the change of key is deferred until nearly the end of the answer. We shall see, as already referred to, that it was a common practice in earlier days to maintain the original tonality far into the answer and even throughout it. Bach's use of this shows his scholarship, his understanding of the habits of thought of those who had gone before him. It also explains away many of the points in his fugues that have been criticized; Bach himself being accused of 'confusing the issue.'

This observation is closely linked to the following:

(viii). Tovey says that

'the question arises whether the alternation between subject and answer is an alternation between *two keys* or an alternation between *two positions of the same scale.*'

I would like to modify this to

'the question arises whether the alternation between subject and answer is an alternation between *two keys* or an alternation between *two positions of the same mode.*' That is, the answer is a diatonic transference not involving modulation, in which case it is clearly seen that differences in the quality of respective intervals in the subject and answer will occur. Bach was fully aware of this.

It is perhaps not necessary to point out that a subject in a mode transferred a fifth higher diatonically is different from a subject in a key transferred a fifth higher diatonically.

It is clear, too, in the following:

Concerning the Dominant in a Mode and the Dominant in a Key

At this juncture some fuller reference to the Modes is essential in order to clear up any confusion that may exist concerning the term 'dominant' as applied to either a Mode or a Scale (modern scale).

In our modern scale the Dominant is a fixed degree of the scale—it is always the fifth degree. (In fact, it gives its name to the fifth degree.)

In the Modes, the Dominant, although fixed for each individual mode, does not fall upon the same degree in all of them. This is shown in the following diagrams:

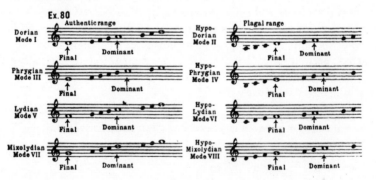

In his book, *Plainsong Accompaniment* (Oxford University Press), J. H. Arnold says:

'Each mode has a dominant, but not in a modern sense, but a dominating note which *asserts itself constantly* in certain melodies of that mode, or acts as a central note around which the melody more or less pivots, though the influence of this note is much stronger in certain classes of melody than in others. The dominant is of supreme importance in the Psalm Tones where it is employed as the reciting note.'

It is clear that the dominant of a mode helped to define that mode next in strength or importance after the Final. Thus in Mode I a subject commencing on the Final (or modern Tonic) would be answered by its dominant.

But if it commenced on A the dominant, it would not be answered by E the fifth above but by D the fourth above:

because D being the Final defines the mode at the very outset, whereas E would not.

Nevertheless, were this being regarded as an answer in A minor to a subject in D minor there is no reason whatever why this E should not be the right note other than the keeping of this modal tradition, because E is to A minor what A is to D minor in our key sense.

Now consider the same thing with regard to Mode VII of which G is the Final (Tonic) and D the dominant.

A subject commencing on the Final would be answered

because D being the dominant defines the mode.

Also would be answered by and not by

because G defines the mode and A does not.

But in Mode VIII, whose Final is G like its authentic Mode VII, if a subject commenced on G it would not be answered by

because this note is not important in this mode, but by

which is the dominant of the mode and defines it. But such an answer could not be considered at all were this regarded as the key of

G major, unless the normal dominant reply were waived for the keeping of this modal one. Let us consider the following excerpt and see if it will help us in this matter of dominants:

'Laudate Dominum' for five voices   Thomas Tallis

If the above is in key C, the first two notes of the Answer are correct. But the following note in the Answer should be F sharp to be in accordance with our ideas of fugal procedure in Keys.

If the above is regarded as beginning in the key G (as at bar 7 there is a perfect cadence in the key G) then the first note of the Answer is wrong —it should be D, the tonic note of the dominant key. The third note should be F sharp.

It is clear that the above reasonings do not solve this matter. The excerpt is not in a key at all. Tallis treated it as in Mode VIII, the Final (or Tonic) of which is G and the dominant C. The modal ear of Tallis naturally answered the final of the mode by its true dominant C and thus defined the mode according to music's own rule. Let us consider the matter further.

At bar 6 the first bass enters with the theme at a higher level—a fifth above the original. This seems quite a correct procedure as at that moment the harmonic circumstance defines a perfect cadence in G. But such a tonality is not maintained, for immediately we see the original answer as in bar 2 (treble) with the F natural. Thus it could be said (1) that the harmonic circumstance establishes G for a moment and controls the

opening of the theme, giving D to G, or (2) that this entry melodically is
an answer with its first note C changed to D. In other words we see here
the Tonic answered by the dominant in mode VII (D) (bar 6) and the
dominant in mode VIII (C) (bar 1). If we regard the matter in this light
it would be no more than saying that the feeling of these two modes was
one and the same tonally, the only difference being their range.[1] This
difference lost force when parts in combination were considered. Two
dominants were available and Tallis used them. When we see that Modes
VII and VIII (the authentic and plagal statements of the same tonality)
become merged into the one scale of G by means of permanent musica
ficta F♯, it may help us to realize that sub-dominantly answered subjects
applied to keys, have only the purpose associated with their use in the
modes, which was to maintain the original tonality for some reasonable
stretch. In our modern keys, sub-dominantly answered subjects—*not
frequent by nature*—are used essentially, to adjust tonality just as in modal
cases, *where by nature they are common*.

In this respect it is interesting to see that Tallis in his 'Laudate Dominum'
maintained tonality by dominantly answering his theme, and that Byrd
achieves the same in his 'Laudate pueri' by sub-dominantly answering
his theme (in both cases the answers are within the mode).

'Laudate pueri'   Byrd

This surely proves that sub-dominantly answered subjects (commonly
called sub-dominant answers) may be used without inventing excuses in
the effort to account for them.

In the light of these observations let us consider the following Organ
Fugue by Bach:

[1] It is important to bear this in mind. We see it in a modern key sense in comparing (a) 'The Blue Bell of Scotland' which is an authentic melody, its range
being between Tonic and Tonic, and (b) the Welsh traditional melody 'Ar hyd y
nos' which is a plagal melody, its range being between dominant and dominant,
but both are in the same major key or scale, and so there is no difference in tonal
feeling.

Prout remarks concerning this:

'Here the answer is in the sub-dominant. The alteration of the semi-tone near the end (B natural answering F natural) is frequently to be met with.'

But the answer is not *in the sub-dominant*; does Prout explain Bach's behaviour here? What guidance does this give to the student?

Is it not a parallel case to Tallis's 'Laudate Dominum'?

The subject is in the same Mode and Bach gives the opening note the same Answer as Tallis, and then continues by treating the Answer *sub-dominantly* WITHIN THE MODE as Byrd does in 'Laudate pueri'. In the modal system the one variable note was B which could be replaced by B flat. Bach understood this and gives us a clear treatment of this subject by his answer. Can there be any doubt of this?

Apropos of this it may be worth while to draw attention to the following quotation from Spitta's *Life of Bach* (Vol. III, page 132):

'It is evident that Bach had evolved from the old church modes a means of expression which he used freely whenever the poetic meaning and musical sequence seemed to him to require it. ... The inexhaustible wealth of harmony which he exhibits ... arises from ... a thorough familiarity with the ecclesiastical modes and an unfailingly keen and certain appreciation of the harmonic relations subsisting in the systems of major and minor.'

Sub-dominantly answered subjects (*Sub-dominant Response*)

In the previous section considering dominants and the answer to the dominant *note*, attention was focused upon the *opening* note of subjects.

Already we have seen not only the dominant note *at or near* the beginning of the subject answered sub-dominantly (as in Tallis's 'Laudate Dominum' and Byrd's 'Laudate pueri'), but also the remainder of the subject; in other words a subject completely answered at the sub-dominant pitch.

We have also seen a subject starting from the Tonic, answered sub-dominantly in full (Bach Fugue, Ex. 84 above—mode VIII type).

Here are a number of examples which show how common was the custom of complete sub-dominant response. Similar instances abound. These examples also illustrate the retention of the original tonality throughout or far into the Answer.

MORLEY (c. 1595) – CANZONET
Ex. 85

PETER PHILLIPS (d. 1628) – SURGENS JESUS
Ex. 86

MUNDI (d. 1591) – RERUM CREATOR OMNIUM
Ex. 87

ANDREA GABRIELLI (d. 1586) – SACERDOS ET PONTIFEX
Ex. 88

PALESTRINA (d. 1594) MISSA BEATA VIRGINE
Ex. 89

PALESTRINA – MISSA REGINA COELI
Ex. 90

No doubt these subjects or ideas were often short, and so it was to some extent essential to retain the original feeling, otherwise there would be no stability of tonality. This would seem to be the reason why Bach in some cases avoids the dominant key until well into the Answer and sometimes throughout it; or merely hints at the dominant key without establishing it by any sense of repose. But the organ fugue (page 74) has a subject by no means short. Again in Byrd's 'Laudate pueri' shortness of subject does not count for much. The motet is for six voices, and the tonality of Mode V (akin to F major) is kept up for thirteen long bars of the kind shown in the excerpt on page 73. After the real answer to the first note of the subject, the remainder is sub-dominantly answered.

Byrd thus maintained the opening tonality for a good stretch, and this was evidently his intention.

It is interesting to see Palestrina at work in the following example:

The subject is answered dominantly throughout but *not in the dominant key* which is avoided; thus the original tonality is undisturbed.

These, and many other examples that could be given, seem to point to the source of Dr. R. O. Morris's observation:

'*Sometimes* the change (of key) is deferred until nearly the end of the Answer as in Bach, Vol. I, 8.'

Evidently the procedure was a common one and not an occasional one in the earlier days.

Further, these examples demonstrate the idea expressed by Dr. Morris when he writes:

'The object of the modification is not primarily to reproduce the subject in the dominant key, but to give its approximate equivalent in the corresponding plagal register.'

We have seen that:

in the immediate answer (where the circumstance was a melodic one) there was adjustment owing to the influence of the dominant note in defining the mode.

This adjustment in *modal compositions* was not limited to the immediate answer, but was generally observed so long as the original tonality was maintained. An answer, apart from this opening dominant note which was more or less isolated, was made dominantly or sub-dominantly, whichever kept the response within the mode (and defined it).

In Tallis's 'Laudate Dominum' we see the lower register of the mode, answered by the upper register in the relation of ⌐ 4th ⌐ and ⌐ 5th ⌐ in Byrd's 'Laudate Pueri' the two registers are ⌐ 5th ⌐ ⌐ 4th ⌐.

Sometimes the response is in the plagal register and sometimes in the authentic, really according to the mode.

But even in so early a work as Tallis's 'Laudate Dominum' the power of harmonic circumstance is felt, and to my mind foreshadows what we see in common practice with Bach (and also Handel). At bar 7 a perfect cadence was established in Key G major. So strong was this that the opening interval (a fourth) of the Subject (though moving from Tonic to Dominant notes) was reproduced as dominant to tonic in the *key*.

Obviously this *dominant chord* is to a *key* what the *dominant note* (not necessarily the fifth) is to a *mode*. They define key and mode respectively.

Thus as key-tonality asserted itself so the defining influence of melody yielded to that of harmony. There were times when, in scalic or key fugues, the dominant note might be answered dominantly (really) in preference to sub-dominantly (tonally), *according as the harmonic or melodic circumstance was the stronger.* So it would seem possible historically and musically to account for TONAL and REAL treatments within the same composition.

We shall see how this is worked out by Bach and if there is method in what he does. It is clear to me that his treatment is based on the same musicianly reasoning as had guided earlier masters. *He usually made a tonal reply in the immediate answer, when a subject began on the dominant, but did not hesitate to make a real reply in later answers where the harmonic circumstance demanded it.*

Consideration of Bach's treatment of CLASS III (subjects which use the dominant note at the beginning)

An examination of Bach's 'Forty-eight' would seem to suggest the following plans: A and B:

PLAN A

When a subject *opens with the dominant note* and *ends in the Tonic key*, the *immediate Answer opens tonally*, that is with the Tonic note of the subject, thus following the old custom of modal subjects and answers. Instances of this are to be seen in the following fugues:

Vol. I, Nos. 3, 7, 11, 13, 16, 21.

Vol. II, Nos. 1, 2, 12, 14, 16, 17, 20, 24.

N.B.—Even if the subject modulates to the dominant key, but by means of a Codetta leads back to the tonic key as in Vol. I, No. 7, the answer opens tonally.

An example or two will suffice:

BACH VOL. I. No. 3

Ex. 92

BACH VOL. II. No. 20

Ex. 93

BACH VOL. I. No. 16

Ex. 94

These examples seem to suggest that the *ending* of the subject may be observed with advantage.

Now although the following examples do not agree with the advice or conclusion as stated in Plan A, yet they do not set it at nought. They can be explained; they are mentioned because they will strengthen the understanding and confidence of the student. Thus the following subject by Bach (*Breitkopf and Haertel Clavierwerke*, Vol. VII, page 80) would appear at first to contradict the above advice; although the subject begins on the dominant note it is immediately answered as the fifth above. But it is not truly a REAL answer, for it is not in the dominant *key*, which it avoids. (It is not an *exact* transposition a fifth above.) The fact is that the subject is answered *dominantly* and keeps *within the mode* exactly parallel to the example 'Super flumina' by Palestrina on page 76. Bach's subject, answered in this manner, preserves the step-wise melodic opening; it also avoids the effect of a repeated note C between the final note of the subject and the first note of the answer as shown at -*ϕ*-:

The application of this old custom of answering a subject dominantly at the outset served to avoid repeated notes at a conspicuous point -*ϕ*-. Thus the following by Bach in *B. and H. Clavierwerke*, Vol. VIII, page 48:

Bach's treatment of later answers

I would draw attention to the fact that the advice given at the head of this section (Plan A) refers to the *immediate* Answer, that is the first Answer, at which point the melodic circumstance may be said to hold sway. It is worth while to consider what happens in later Answers when the melodic circumstance is outweighed by the harmonic.

In the C♯ major fugue, Vol. I, 3, we discover the opening dominant note being answered at bar 10 quite freely; in fact, its place is taken by two semiquavers neither of which can be regarded as answering the opening quaver of the subject. This is a kind of variance which Bach considers to fulfil a purpose; the impulsive counterpoint already felt in bar 9 is allowed to pursue its course without hindrance. It leads into the entry of the Answer adroitly. It is clear that Bach did not intend a tonal response as the harmony at this point is dominant.

At the *first* appearance of the Answer we see the normal tonal response:

In the G minor fugue, Vol. I, 16, we find two successive appearances of the Answer in bars 13 and 15. The first is tonal, the second is real. The reason is obvious. It is a matter of harmonic circumstance.

These examples indicate clearly enough that Bach did not hesitate to use Real Answers, and that he had no preference for Tonal Answers merely as such. But I would beg leave to quote the example from his Organ fugue in G major, for this cannot fail to convince us that when the harmonic circumstance prevailed Bach used the *Real* response to the opening dominant note. There was no haphazard, unreasoned procedure.

The immediate Answer is Tonal and quite normal.

By the time the fourth strand appears on the pedals, a codetta has carried the music from the tonic key to the dominant chord of the dominant key D. Here Bach uses a Real Answer, for the harmonic circumstance is the prevailing one.

PLAN B

When a Subject *opens with the dominant note* and *modulates to the dominant key or is taken to it by a codetta*:
the immediate Answer follows the custom of being Tonal.

In *later* Answers Bach resorts to treatments similar to those mentioned under Plan A. He appears to use Real or Tonal response according to the artistic demands of the moment. If by retaining tonal response the linear aspect or flow is better, then Bach uses the tonal response (see Ex. 102 below). But if the harmonic circumstance seems sufficiently purposeful he does not hesitate to alter the opening dominant note of the subject itself! This is to be seen in the final section of the Fugue in E flat, Vol. I, No. 7 (see Ex. 105 below).

Here at the immediate Answer Bach retains the customary Tonal response. The *real response* is quite possible at this first answer.

But Bach keeps the tradition. Later Answers do not call forth this Real response, for the Tonal one is better, allowing an unbroken flow; whereas the Real response causes a repetition, and spoils the linear aspect.

In Ex. 105, the immediate answer gives a tonal opening, and later answers follow the same plan. But a somewhat unusual occurrence is seen in the

final section. Here the Answer appears first and is Tonal. It is followed by two bars of episode which lead into the subject. This, by the harmonic circumstance fitting the purpose, takes upon itself a Tonal guise! And why not?

Another similar case occurs at bar 38 of the fugue, Vol. I, 24, where the subject takes upon itself a *Tonal guise* (as the answer) by dropping its original dominant note.

Such cases, viewed in their true perspective, should be regarded as examples of fine craftsmanship and discerning artistry, not irregularities which some would have us regard as unpardonable musical sins.

It might be added that Bach is free of harmonic obligation at the very outset of his instrumental fugues when the *immediate* answer is made, and less free of it when the various strands have entered (unless for some purpose he has arranged otherwise as we shall see in Vol. I, No. 24). This is borne out in our findings for though Bach makes a Tonal answer at the outset, conforming to the old melodic definition of tonality, nevertheless he may use a Real answer later, yielding to harmonic definition.

In the following example from Handel, the fugue is *accompanied*, harmony being associated with the subject from the beginning; thus there is harmonic definition and obligation which settles the immediate Answer as a Real one. Bach would not have been at variance with Handel in this; in such a case he would not have shown any preference for a Tonal answer, for it would have been contrary to his reasoning.

In the following fugue (Vol. I, No. 24) which is the only other instance in the '48' of a subject commencing on the dominant note and modulating to the dominant key, Bach designs to avoid any Real answer throughout its whole course.

The immediate answer is tonal, the dominant note being replied to by the tonic.

It can readily be seen that were the answer to enter *above* the subject, a real answer would be imperative as only two voices are concerned (the interval of the fourth being discordant).

It is interesting to see therefore what occurs during the progress of the fugue. Bach chose the tonal response by definitely postponing his answers to a suitable point of entry. This is seen when the fourth strand enters above the counter-subject; by means of a codetta Bach brings the music away from F sharp minor to B minor and so a tonal entry is invited, or made possible.

THE ANSWER

In a manner similar to this Bach maintains the Tonal response throughout the fugue, but this does not provide grounds for saying that Bach had definite preference for tonal answers!

A consideration of Bach's treatment of CLASS IV (when answering subjects which use the dominant note NEAR THE BEGINNING *of the subject)*

Eight subjects occur in the '48' which have the dominant note near the beginning more or less prominently placed.

In every case the FIRST or immediate Answer is Tonal.

The fugues are Vol. I, Nos. 2, 8, 17, 22, 23, and Vol. II, Nos. 7, 11, 21. These fugue subjects all remain in the Tonic key.

The reason for Bach's treatment, consistent indeed, cannot fail to bring to mind the *modal tradition* to which, already, attention has been strongly drawn (see page 70 *et seq.*). In those earlier days the Answer was a *Diatonic response within the mode*, and a complete answer *sub-dominantly* was common. Thus the retaining of the opening tonality for quite a period, as seen in the examples provided on pages 72 *et seq.*, was natural. When the Answer came, under later tonality, to be generally a transposition of the subject into the dominant key and not merely *diatonically at the fifth above*, the retaining of the original tonality was not quite the natural procedure, but nevertheless *there was no need to abandon it.* There was really nothing exceptional about it and we shall see that its purpose with Bach was as clear as with those earlier musicians. It is only exceptional and puzzling to those who for some reason have not been able to account for it.

We are reminded too of the following quotation from Dr. Dent's *Fugue for Beginners*:

> 'An old rule which modern text-books have forgotten is that when the subject ends in the tonic it must carefully avoid an obvious move to the dominant in order that the answer may enter,'

which is surely coincident with the observation of Dr. R. O. Morris (page 67 (m)):

> 'sometimes the change of key is deferred until nearly the end of the Answer.'

In all the eight examples from Bach, *there is no codetta or link between subject and answer*. The subjects all remain in the Tonic key, so that the Answer enters without any preparation having been made to lead into the dominant key.

If, therefore, the dominant note is answered by its dominant it may cause an *obvious move* to the dominant key. The spirit of the early custom in maintaining the original tonality well into the answer and even throughout it, *is seen to apply to the examples we are considering with true musical fitness. The maintaining of the tonic tonality well into the answer is the crux of the matter and holds priority of importance and is the deciding factor. It is the application of an old custom.*

Examine these eight examples from Bach's '48' carefully, and in the light of the above observations Bach's procedure will present no difficulty whatever; instead of some of them being regarded as exceptional, it will be seen that they are truly normal. (Special reference will be made to some of these quotations later.) The asterisks indicate the dominant note in the subject and the response to it in the answer.

This brings us to an end of the present consideration of Bach's treatment of the dominant *note* (either at or near the opening of the fugue subject) in the Answer. *On account of the criticisms launched against Bach's Answers in several of the above cases,* a fuller explanation of them must be made, but before doing this we will make reference to the works of our English composer, Henry Purcell.

A brief consideration of the fugal writing of Henry Purcell

We shall carry out this examination of Purcell's fugal writing in order to see if Purcell knew and respected the customs and freedoms of his predecessors as revealed in their works from which quotations have already been made.

Excerpts will be taken from the Fantasias for Strings (1680) and from the Sonatas of Four Parts (Two violins, Bassus and Harpsichord or Organ) published in 1697, two years after his death. These Sonatas were written at periods dating later than that of the Fantasias.

In the historical preface to these Fantasias (published by Curwen), Peter Warlock says of them:

'Assuredly we must go forward to Bach before we can find any music which displays such consummate mastery of all the devices of counterpoint allied to so wide a range of profoundly expressive harmony. It is in these early Fantasias modelled on the old English tradition that he shows his greatest originality and finest musicianship, though the Sonatas composed later, in which he tells us "he has faithfully endeavoured a just imitation of the most famed Italian masters", no doubt seemed to his contemporaries far more modern and up to date.'

Here are two quotations from Fantasia No. 1:

This is in Mode I, but soars into amazing harmony as it proceeds. The short theme begins on the Final of the Mode and is answered *dominantly* as was natural.

This also shows *sub-dominant answers*, and much freedom in many ways. Note that the opening note D being the final of the mode is answered dominantly by A according to the mode, but the remainder of the theme is answered at the fourth above, sub-dominantly (see also Ex. 82 from Byrd, page 73).

Now follow a number of quotations from the Sonatas of Four Parts. Although 'Imitating the famed Italian masters', note the strong Modal character of Purcell's work. Of all the works which have gained for Purcell so high a place among musicians, I do not think any would impress the earnest student more than these Fantasias and Sonatas. They show consummate skill and harmonic daring such as place him by the side of Bach.

Observations

The 2nd violin answers the opening note of the 1st violin, *tonally*, according to custom, but the rest of the theme is answered *dominantly* as regards *pitch*, but *diatonically* as regards tonality. Here we see Purcell maintaining the tonality of the subject throughout the Answer, as his predecessors so often did, and, as we have already seen, Bach did not hesitate to do. The dominant key of F♯ minor is not touched until the end of the third entry and even then it has the Picardy third.

The notes 'bracketed' should be carefully considered in pairs as marked, for they speak for themselves. (Compare this with Bach, Vol. II, No. 21, bars 5 and 21.)

This illustrates a real response, a transposition of the subject into the dominant key and is quite normal. *The subject has no modal feeling.*

This is an interesting case because the dominant note * in the subject is answered tonally; and this causes the two preceding notes also to have sub-dominant response. The reason is clear—there was the object of keeping within the Tonic Tonality throughout the Answer as was so common —this is clearly shown too at the cadence ⌐‾‾⌐ which avoids G♯ the leading note in A minor, and also by the C♯ at the same point. It is worth while comparing the response in this case with the response in the previous example, for both themes descend from Tonic note to Dominant note. In both cases the opening tonic note is answered dominantly—but whereas in the first case the dominant note is answered dominantly (and its two preceding notes), in the second case the corresponding notes are answered *sub*-dominantly, after which the remainder of the theme is dominantly answered. The difference in treatment is entirely due to the fact that in the first case there was no demand from a tonality point of view that the tonic key should be further maintained; the move into the dominant key was not *obvious*—in other words there was no abruptness, forcing the dominant tonality upon the ear. In the second case we see a modal custom carried out very definitely.

Here it will be seen that after the opening tonic notes have been answered dominantly, the rest of the subject is answered *sub-dominantly*. *The subject itself ended in the dominant key*, and an answer such as this was used by Bach, and we have already seen how common was the sub-dominant response in earlier days. The treatment is all in keeping with tradition and musical sense.

This is another minor key subject, but it *does not modulate*, and it is answered normally, at the fifth above (fourth below). The dominant note occurs prominently, but it is *not* answered by the tonic. A glance at the fourth bar shows clearly that a tonal answer here would be as difficult as it is unessential.

The above shows a technique in full accordance with that of earlier days—see Tallis's *Laudate Dominum*, p. 72, Byrd's *Laudate Pueri*, p. 73. The subject is restated two octaves below in the Bass and then followed by a *Tonal* response (x) which holds the music to the Tonic key until the very end of the Answer which defines the key of G major. This is immediately followed by a *second* Answer (y), but this time *Real* from the outset. Thus by means of the Tonal response (x) the Tonic tonality is carried to the close of the first Answer, and quite a good stretch has been made in the Tonic key, aided too by the restatement of the Subject to begin with. At (y), however, the dominant key is established and the harmonic circumstance calls for a Real response. Surely this shows us the *freedom* of the musician as artist and craftsman; it is as clear as daylight what Byrd, Tallis, Purcell and their like were about; we see music shaping her own laws.

This brief investigation gives proof that Purcell's technique was in direct line with that of the early modal composers. This technique (as we have already seen) was known and respected by J. S. Bach. He applied it to his fugues which as music are more remote than Purcell's from modal influence. *Thus the gap was bridged between mode and key.* It is clear that when these fugal movements are being examined, *the full exposition, and not merely the immediate context—the answer—must be taken into consideration if we wish to discover the reason for the procedure.* It is exactly the same with Bach as with Purcell. The musician's ear and mind are at work and if, in examining these works, we go no further than the Answer, we are likely to be led to false conclusions. We shall find ourselves accusing these master-musicians of errors which do not exist. This leads us on to a study of

THE ANSWER

Bach's (so-called) Inconsistencies

The following examples from Bach, upon which authors have felt themselves bound to pass judgment, we will examine in the light of our study in the present chapter.

One author, having explained the tonal opening, continues:

'If, however, the leap to the dominant at the outset can be regarded as a good $\frac{6}{4}$ the answer *can* be real. *But Bach shows no consistency in the matter.* For example, here are the subject and answer of an Organ fugue. The Answer could have been tonal, but it is equally good as a real one.'

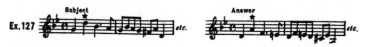

As one sees, Bach gives a real answer. *But in doing so he shows no inconsistency.*

It was pointed out on page 83 that in all the eight cases in the '48' where a dominant note near the beginning of the subject was answered tonally, the reason was to maintain Tonic tonality for a space after the Answer had entered. There was purpose in this, because the dominant key had not been reached, and a real answer would have disturbed or interfered with the smooth flow in the Tonic key and would have drawn attention to the move towards the dominant key. But the present case is quite different. There is no need for a Tonal Answer. Already the key of the dominant has been hinted at by the codetta (see Ex. 36) and no purpose would be served by melodic adjustment. The dominant key is being smoothly entered. Even if a Tonal answer had been chosen by Bach he could still have used a Dominant harmony $\sharp$ ^{6}$_2$ on G amounting to the same thing as a real answer. Obviously Bach is consistent. The old modal system retained the original tonality throughout the Answer by nature; the bringing in of musica ficta, creating a perfect cadence in the dominant, was *delayed* often to the end of the exposition *on purpose* to maintain a smooth tonal flow for a stretch. The same purpose is behind the procedure of Purcell and Bach.

The present case of Bach is really parallel to the following by Purcell:

A careful study of the above will show how a tonal treatment of the subject would produce a fidgety harmonic patch instead of the broad Tonic and Dominant basis of the first bar.

Exactly for the same basic reason—the maintaining of smooth tonal flow or steadiness of tonality—the following cases show *tonal* answers:

The tonality of the Tonic key is maintained—undisturbed—well into the Answer and the change to G minor is gradual, not forced or obvious. But Dr. Kitson says of the two cases just quoted that:

'The answers are tonal, but to be consistent they should be real.'

I think it is clear enough that Bach's procedure is not only correct, but also the best musical one, and that he *is* consistent, working according to musical tradition as well as musicianly reasoning.

The same reasoning concerning the maintenance of tonality and delay of modulation can be applied to the following examples, and no doubt the student will find others.

I would refer the student to comments upon the first of these examples by Dr. Kitson in his book, *The Elements of Fugal Construction* (page 39).

Regarding the second of the above examples, Dr. Prout (*Fugue*) offers the following explanation:

'So strongly is the leading note felt as the third of the dominant that it is not seldom answered by the third of the tonic, *even when there is no modulation*. Here Bach treats the second and third notes of a subject as the third and sixth of E, and answers them by the third and sixth of A, *though the subject ends in the key of the tonic.*'

The italics are mine. I would ask—'Can a leading note be felt as the third of the dominant when there is no modulation to that key? Can such reasoning be of help to a student? Can there be guidance based upon wishful explanation?'

The same author says:

'The same principles will guide us in dealing with the leading note. *Let the fundamental principle be thoroughly grasped that the tonal change must be made as soon as possible, and the whole thing is easy. If* the subject modulates, the leading note must always be treated as the third of the dominant and answered by the third of the tonic.'

The following example is then given with the remark that it shows the leading note F double sharp very early in the subject treated as the third of the dominant and answered by the third of the tonic. The following notes of the subject are all answered as belonging to the dominant key:

BACH '48' VOL. I. No.18
Subject

Ex.133   Answer

Let us consider Prout's theory.

First of all, the subject does *not* modulate in the first bar—by no possible musical reasoning can the first bar be regarded as being in D♯ minor. So the theory about the leading note does not apply. Again the third of the Tonic is a minor third B♮, and not a major one.

However, this little bit of grit in the wheel of explanation is ingeniously removed by Stewart Macpherson who, in his *Studies in the Art of Counterpoint*, goes so far as to say:

'Here the leading note of G♯ minor is regarded as the major third of the dominant key, and answered by the major third of the Tonic.'

I would ask—can this possibly satisfy the earnest student? What guidance does it offer him? To me it seems to reach the limit to which a false idea can be forced.

Dr. R. O Morris (see p. 67 (n)) says in regard to this same fugue subject:

'there are many modulating subjects which cannot be answered in accordance with the above rules[1] without undue distortion. In such cases *it is best to take the bull by the horns and give a real answer in the sub-dominant.*'

Apparently the sub-dominant answer has only to be resorted to in cases of extreme difficulty and awkwardness.

Bach, as we see, did give a real answer in the sub-dominant key (after the first note), but in doing so did he think he was resorting to such measures as taking the bull by the horns? I cannot imagine this to be the case.

In using the sub-dominant response Bach was not only musically right, but was doing what Purcell and earlier fugal masters had done before him (see p. 73 *et seq.*). The sub-dominant response, even when diatonic according to the mode, served to keep the theme and answer bounded by a limited tonality (often the one tonality), and it served this purpose with Palestrina and Purcell (see p. 87, Sonata 4) as here with Bach. Bach followed an old custom based on musical sense, and in transferring it from mode to key did so without compunction, without thought of apology, for it was not a last resort, but a common and appropriate procedure. This surely should help us to do away with the idea that Bach had a strong preference for the Tonal Answer. He had no such preference merely as a personal fad; he was a scholar; he was first and last a musician, and it was the music that mattered.

Now let us turn our attention to the fugue which has been the object of much discussion. As it is essential to have the music before our eyes, we will quote not only the Subject and Answer, but the complete Exposition.

Ex.134

BACH '48' VOL.I. No. 23

[1] That is, the rules which this author gives concerning Tonal Answers.

92

The point at issue is—Why did Bach give a sub-dominant answer to the notes within the bracket x ▭ ?

Prout merely says that it shows

'the leading note very early in the subject treated as the third of the dominant, and answered by the third of the tonic. The following notes of the subject are all answered as belonging to the dominant key.'

But this statement does not satisfy the student who cannot see why in this particular case the Answer should be anything other than straightforward; it is nothing more than an attempt to tell us what we can see for ourselves.

Stewart Macpherson says:

'So remarkably does Bach manifest this preference[1] that he sometimes treats the leading note in this way, even when the Subject does *not* actually modulate to the Dominant Key.'

He also adds in a footnote:

'Here he [Bach] evidently feels the A♯ in the subject so strongly as the third of the dominant harmony [F♯, A♯, C♯] that he prefers to answer all three of them by the corresponding notes of the tonic harmony.'

Does this offer any help whatever towards our understanding of Bach's purpose?

Sir Edward Bairstow says:[2]

'If either a real or a tonal answer is possible, the tonal answer is generally more satisfactory because it presents variety, and in some curious way does seem to give an "answer" to the question asked by the subject. Bach's No. 23 Book I would normally be regarded as being entirely in B and would have a real answer.'

Ex.135

Continuing he adds:

'Bach took the unusual view that the notes under the bracket x (in the subject) were in F♯ and thus arrived at the tonal answer.'

[1] The following note by Macpherson is given in connexion with points referring to the answering of a modulating subject: 'Most of the great fugal writers, notably Bach himself, often prefer to think of the *leading note as the third of the dominant key*, rather than as the seventh of the tonic key, and to answer it by the third of the tonic key, not by the seventh of the dominant.'

[2] In *Counterpoint and Harmony*, E. C. Bairstow (Macmillan & Stainer & Bell), compare Palestrina 'Super Flumina', p. 76.

I would ask—was Bach's view unusual? If so, the student is anxious to know why it entered Bach's mind, and on what lines he was working.

Why did Bach choose to give the answer shown in Ex. 134?

I would suggest that in this procedure he was preserving the original (the Tonic) tonality not only well into the Answer, but beyond—just as his predecessors had done, as is shown by Palestrina (see p. 75, *Missa Regina Coeli*), and by Byrd (see p. 73, *Laudate Pueri*) and by Tallis (see p. 72, *Laudate Dominum*) and by Purcell (see p. 88, Sonata No. 7, *vivace*).

A close examination not only shows this to be so, but reveals the *whole exposition* as a parallel to Tallis's *Laudate Dominum* and many similar cases where a *change of tonality was delayed until the ending of the subject in the last voice.*

Reference to the Exposition shows that the first answer merely touches upon the dominant key at (a)—it has the effect of colouring rather than modulation, for there is no strong cadence point, nor does the answer end with a perfect cadence in the dominant key; in fact, such a cadence is deliberately avoided (b). Thus Bach shows that he is intentionally maintaining tonic tonality, and this is further supported by the fact that it is only at the close of the Exposition (as the fourth voice finishes) that the perfect cadence in the dominant key fully establishes modulation (c). Surely no better comparison with the early customs could be desired. Palestrina, Tallis, Byrd, Purcell and Bach were truly masters of their craft—and their methods show their insight as musicians. And is it not clear that their thought was altogether beyond and outside such considerations as whether or not the leading note should be regarded as the third of the dominant? Such arguments serve to show that theorists never considered the *whole exposition* which alone could give them the clue. They were content to look no further than the Answer and devise some pseudo-explanation which has served only to confuse the student more and more.

Now let us examine the Fugue in B♭, Vol. II, 21.

Here, too, the whole exposition must be given.

BACH '48' VOL. II. No. 21

Ex. 136

Redundant Answer

Dr. Kitson says of this Answer that

'Bach seems to have confused the issue.'

But if we are patient to look beyond the immediate Answer and examine the whole exposition as in the case of Vol. I, 23, we shall find that Bach's treatment and his reason for it reveal a mind which is crystal clear. There is nothing which indicates confusion in *Bach's* mind.

To begin with the third note of the Answer does not reproduce the interval of the subject at that point. The Answer has a tone, the subject a semitone. This entirely agrees with the work of all the earlier writers already quoted: Palestrina (*Super flumina*), Tallis (*Laudate Dominum*) Purcell (Sonata 1, *Canzona*).

The Answer is a diatonically conceived one, keeping within the key, as earlier writers kept within the mode. There is no question of 'confusing the issue'. (This matter of the Answer not reproducing the quality of the intervals in the subject will be mentioned again a little later, p. 96). The first Answer is tonal, the dominant note F being answered by B♭, and it is only in the latter half of the Answer that the dominant key of F is touched; even then only by an inverted perfect cadence which is very short lived. Obviously Bach's intention was to maintain the Tonic key well into the Answer. A Codetta follows in the space of which the sub-dominant key of E♭ enters into the conversation; then, at bar 13, the subject appears in the Bass in the tonic key again. After this a short codetta really establishes the dominant key at which point a redundant Answer occurs in the Bass, bar 21. As the dominant key is already established, there is no purpose in preserving the key of the subject B♭ as when the first answering voice entered. So there is no need for the tonal response and the B♭ as in bar 5, nor is there any need for E♭ (the third note of the first Answer). Bach here gives a full Real Answer, again following the practice and musicianship of earlier composers. In the light of this, can anyone maintain that Bach 'confused the issue'?

Another case in which Bach's procedure has been much debated is the last fugue in volume one.

BACH VOL. I. No. 24

Ex.137

Here is Bach's answer:

Ex.138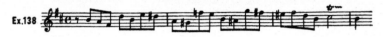

Dr. Kitson says:

'This is really a case in which it would have been *possible* to commence the answer in the key of the sub-dominant.'

Here is Dr. Kitson's suggested answer beginning in the sub-dominant:

Ex.139

The answer to this subject has already been discussed (see p. 82). Bach's answer cannot be mistaken for a statement of the subject (as distinct from answer), whereas Dr. Kitson's coincides with the statement of the Subject in E minor. Thus although Bach must use a tonal answer which, apart from the second, third and fourth notes, coincides with Dr. Kitson's, yet by recognizing the dominant key as far as possible, he identifies such a result with an Answer and not a Subject. Bach begins with a tonal response to the first note, F♯, and follows this by a real response to the next three notes, D, B and G, giving A, F♯ and D, that is the three notes which are characteristic of F♯ minor, the dominant key. After the first four notes (see Ex. 138) the subject is answered *sub-dominantly*. Besides, as the subject ends in the key of F♯ minor, it is a simpler matter musically to link this up with the answer as Bach gives it. Can there be any doubt as to the musical wisdom of Bach's reply? The student will surely turn to this fugue and the G♯ minor one (Vol. I, No. 18) on many occasions, for guidance concerning *subdominantly-answered* subjects.

On p. 95 attention was drawn to the matter of the answer not reproducing the quality of the corresponding intervals in the subject. Dr. Kitson, after saying that

'A correct answer is always at the interval of a perfect fifth or fourth from the subject'

remarks that

'Bach sometimes uses the diatonic lower auxiliary note, thus causing a divergence from the principle in unessentials.'

THE ANSWER

As examples of this he quotes:

But is not Bach following Palestrina and Purcell, making a diatonic response within the mode, as already referred to? Obviously he knew all about such customs.

Dr. Kitson continues:

'And cases could be quoted in which there seems to be no valid reason for the breach of the principle'

and says that Prout quotes the following case among others:

Prout's remark about it is:

'Though as a general rule the transposition of the subject a perfect fourth or fifth should be strictly carried out, we often find the position of semitones disregarded, a semitone being answered by a tone and a tone by a semitone. This is especially the case with the sub-dominant and leading note.'

But this does not explain the why and the wherefore. Dr. Kitson says:

'It is difficult to say why the Answer should not have been given thus':

In Bach's Answer it will be noticed that the first and last notes are the normal reply to a Tonic, A being answered by E.

It should also be observed that the rest of the Answer is *not* in the sub-dominant *key*. What is the explanation? Is it not clear that the Answer is a diatonic response within the mode, within the scale? Is it not another example of a subject answered diatonically and *sub-dominantly (but not in the sub-dominant key)* thus maintaining the original tonality, as was the common practice of the earlier masters?

97

This chapter might be brought to a close by an example (from the 48) of a subject which ends on a *factor of the dominant chord* of the Tonic key, but not *in* the dominant key.

It will be seen that Bach's Answer is a Real one and ends on the dominant chord in its own key; whereas, had the dominant chord terminated the subject and marked the establishment of the dominant *key*, the Answer would have been Tonal, and would have ended in the Tonic key. One should notice how appropriately Bach uses a codetta to bridge over the gap from this point to the entry of the subject in the Tonic key again.

To the skilful building of this codetta, reference has already been made.

.   .   .   .

Although a text-book of this kind is not the place to indulge in exhaustive investigation, yet I venture to hope that sufficient has been done by means of this historical approach to cast a clearer light upon Bach's examples and show them in their true perspective.

Chapter Six

THE EXPOSITION

The exposition—as its name implies—exposes, lays before us, the essential thematic resource of the fugue. The subject is the 'fons et origo' of the whole composition. The themes, often spoken of as counter-points or counter-subjects, which go with it later, are in one sense at any rate not 'counter' at all; they are its good companions. Thus the exposition of a three-part fugue provides three strands of potential musical material. I say 'potential' because students commonly appear not to realize or understand that counter-subjects (or even free parts) must be valuable essential matter; or, through lack of experience, fail to make them so. And so their fugue embarks on its course unpromisingly, with an exposition of no vital consequence, because the strands of it have little or nothing to offer.

Let us come to concrete facts about these strands which make up the exposition; let us see what constitutes potential material. We will examine the strands of an exposition, one by one, and we need not open our '48' beyond the second fugue. Here is the first strand, the one which starts off, announcing and pursuing its course throughout the three-part exposition.

And here is the second strand, starting with the Answer and continuing to the end of the exposition.

How many students look upon their strand-making in this way?

Now here is the third strand which is merely the subject itself in the bass making the third entry; but to give a fair and true idea we must also show the first and second strands above it, all three continuing and carrying on their work—one might say their duties—together.

Ex.147

What an interesting and perfect texture these strands make! These two bars, the subject with its two counter-subjects, mark the climax of the exposition, showing the strands, previously isolated, in combination. They indicate the power and function of these three separate voices, in the making of which Bach had in mind their combined effectiveness. They define or at least forecast the possibilities and probabilities of the fugue; in a word they are its essence. But let us cast our eyes carefully over the exposition written out in full.

Ex.148

What points can we note and learn from it?

(i). That the strands do not lose interest when looked at individually—they maintain purpose even within themselves.

(ii). That the strands are not mere commotion, more or less restless or haphazard—they are *ordered* movement.

(iii). That the first and second strands do not in any degree strive or vie with each other in the way of activity; they consider each other and leave room too for the third strand; all three enjoy complementary conversation.

All these points are elemental in their importance; but there are others to note.

(iv). That the first and second strands form double counterpoint; both are good basses.

(v). That all three strands form triple counterpoint; all are correct as basses.

These two facts possess far-reaching significance: Number (iv) is essential, speaking with the examination test in mind. Number (v) is undoubtedly a valuable asset.

Double and Triple Counterpoint

Triple counterpoint is an inestimable part of fugal equipment, and as there is no reason for the student with musical gumption to fear it, I see no purpose in delaying the study of it. I strongly recommend students to practise it at every opportunity, for it is *experience* backed by an alert mind that counts. The one who has schooled himself in double counterpoint can, with further application of mind, reap the value of triple counterpoint. Instructions may be found in books by esteemed teachers, but above all the student should study Bach.

In thus far examining the exposition we have observed points that can hardly fail to influence our own efforts. But the student asks, seeing Bach's perfect work, how is it done? What is the method of attack, of setting about it? Is there a secret? If there is a secret, it is surely an open one, and declared in the exposition before us.

First of all place the subject in the bass.

Add above it the first counter-subject (C.S. I), making good two-part harmony as well as good counterpoint and capable of being a true bass. Test this as you write it by placing it also *below* the subject; if there are faults they should be detected at this moment and not later on when trouble has been caused.

Then above these two strands add the second counter-subject (C.S. II), and test it as you write it , in the same way as C.S. I was tested.

This is the musician's *craft*; it remains for him to imbue it with *artistry*, and this aspect of the work was spoken of in Chapter III, 'The Counter-subject'.

Even at this early stage of the career of the fugue, it is convincingly clear that dry bones are no use. Every note must be as delicately chosen and weighed as words and syllables are by the poet; for a fugue is poetry. And as far as fugue is concerned there have been many poetasters and too few poets.

Further Points

But there are still more points which we should note in this exposition. Let us regard it especially from the aspect of the potential matter that these strands afford. Do they contain ideas which invite further consideration?

(vi). The opening cluster of notes ♫♫♪ arrests attention immediately. Even ♫♪ has possibilities.

Ex.149

(vii). The scalic link, continuing the subject into the C.S. in bar 3, at once attracts our notice.

Ex.150

Both these ideas, (vi) and (vii), are of an active type.

(viii). The counter-subject contains a group of notes *less active* than either (vi) or (vii). It follows the scalic link (vii) and persists throughout the counter-subject; it invites our attention as a contrast to the more active ideas.

Ex.151

All these ideas we have discovered in the subject or counter-subject. But the exposition also includes an important codetta covering bars 5 and 6, and there we find an assertive series of upward-moving semiquavers in the lower strand, which seems to say, 'You'll hear of me again'.

Ex.152

Looked at more closely we shall see it is written in double-counterpoint against the other strand, a fact that is quite suggestive of further use.

Such are the treasures that lie like precious stones embedded in this exposition. But they did not fall there by accident. Bach's own hand, directed by his mind, placed them there. We have now seen the kind of 'stuff that fugues are made on'—good fugues, of course; and having discovered such potential material, the still greater joy is to watch Bach at work with it as the fugue expands; but this we must postpone for a little while.

In a book of small dimensions, it is not possible to give minute examination—on these lines—of even a dozen expositions chosen from the '48'; nor would our prime purpose be served by doing so. No doubt, the student whose interest is aroused will, at his leisure, do some browsing over other expositions and see what they hold in store. But at first it may be wise to study only a few of them and do that study thoroughly.

The Codetta

The Codetta may well serve a double purpose, as this Exposition shows. It will be remembered that in the chapter on The Codetta it was pointed out that the codetta space between the Answer and the return of the Subject not only offered greater scope than the earlier one between Subject and Answer, but that it was also more generally present in a Fugue. Not only does it serve (especially in Minor keys) to bridge over the return to the tonic key in a graceful manner, avoiding any feeling of obvious modulation, but may and generally should provide further material which may be called upon in the expansion of the fugue.

The student, therefore, when planning his exposition, will be wise to bear this in mind.

Some general observations

(a) *The tonic note of the subject is responded to by the tonic note in the key of the Answer, usually the Dominant.* Students are rather prone to think that the tonic note in the key of the Answer must be accompanied by a factor of its own triad; for instance, that G (answering C) must be a factor of the chord of G, and the subject (or first strand) must at that point have reached a factor of that chord also. An illustration from Bach's '48' will make this clear.

The note G at -ϕ- is not accompanied by a factor of the chord of G. One can imagine a student adding a codetta reaching the key of G at that point where the Answer might enter somewhat as follows:

which is not wrong; but he might have done this under the impression that by the time the Answer makes its entry, it was imperative to have reached the dominant key.

This matter, though perhaps appearing a little trivial at first sight, might well be followed up; the student should examine all the examples occurring in the '48' namely: Vol. I, 4, 5, 8, 14, 23, and 24. Vol. II, 4, 5, 6, 7, 9, 19, 22, and 23.

He will find that many of them are worthy of much more than a glance. I cannot refrain from quoting from one or two, and, did space permit, would quote more.

There is nothing calling for special attention in this, but it reminds us that a bare fifth makes a good start in two-part counterpoint.

This is a case which the student should be able to explain without hesitation (the tonic key being maintained well into the Answer).

Quite apart from the immediate point of interest at the entry of the Answer—and who but Bach would have done it so?—is the modification of the end of the Answer where the tierce de picardie is used (A♮). This shows that such procedure was not eschewed by Bach, but was used with musical advantage when the occasion suited him. It should be carefully noted. The codetta too is full of colour and is clearly framed on the basis of sequence. Codettas returning from the Answer to the Subject in Minor key expositions touch upon the relative major key of the subject at times as in fugues Vol. II, 20 and 24. Such observations are worth noting and the student should scour the whole '48'.

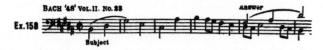

These four examples are of interest, and will increase the student's resource if he is not the sort to be content with merely reading.

THE EXPOSITION

In the examples just referred to the Answer has made its entry *above* the continuing subject. Here are a few in which the Answer makes its entry *below* the continuing subject, but there is no link or codetta; the answer enters without any delay.

The expositions of all these examples would repay the student who troubles to look them up.

(b) Students are apt to show awkwardness in such a thing as passing from the subject in the tonic minor to the entry of the first answer in the Dominant minor. Here are two simple examples from Bach showing that the dominant chord of the new key is not a necessity.

The old tonic F sharp is regarded as sub-dominant in the key of the Answer; it is also the case in the following:

On p. 104 (Ex. 157) reference was made to Bach's use of the tierce de picardie at the end of the Answer in a minor-key fugue. This chord is the dominant of the *tonic* key and so leads back at once, if desired, to the entry of the subject. But although this dominant chord finally ushers in the subject again, it is not essential to create the tierce de picardie at the end of the Answer. The Answer may end in its own key—the dominant minor—and lead by means of a codetta back to the tonic minor gradually. This is the case in the fugue under our attention, Vol. II, No. 12. Thus:

Bach's codettas are a fascinating and no less illuminating study.

Chapter Seven

THE FIRST EPISODE

Reference to the third episode. The use of sequence and figure-development. Interchangeable counterpoint. Interchangeable counterpoint with interchange in the same episode. The double-prong episode.

The second decision concerning the lay-out of the fugue (p. 23) was that the first episode should be written showing sequential repetition, possibly extended by means of figure-development, with a part against it in double-counterpoint, or parts against it in triple-counterpoint, or parts in double-counterpoint together with a free part.

Let us consider

THREE-STRAND FUGUES

and in doing so let us in each case note two things in particular:

(a) The *material or idea* which is the germ of the episode.

(b) The *way* this material is used to produce the episode.

I. Bach's Fugue in C minor, Vol. I, No. 2.

One cannot do better than continue the study of this fugue, the exposition of which was examined in Chapter VI.

The following extract shows the end of the exposition (A) in C minor merging into the episode which covers bars 3-5, where the subject enters in the relative major key of E♭ (B).

THE FIRST EPISODE

The music winds along naturally and apparently inevitably. A design is being woven just as we might see on a weaver's loom. What would *you* have done after the close of the Exposition at A? What has Bach done?

The material or idea of the episode is a combination of the opening half-bar figure of the subject and the counter-subject which goes with it.

Bach concentrates on the bass part which contains the movement, attracts the attention and becomes the essence of the episode. The descending semiquaver figure ▬▬▬, etc., which is the opening half-bar of the counter-subject, has been allowed to follow its bent. We see Counterpoint, not hedged in by rules of the systematized species, but going about its expressive busy-ness and achieving artistic purpose. Against these sequentially-repeated half-bar flights occurs the opening germ of the subject, also sequentially repeated. It is shared between the soprano and the alto, and is imitative work (or might be regarded as canonic). The modulation from C minor to E♭ major is clear and does not force itself upon the ear.

The episode is made by the sequential repetition of two ideas which are in interchangeable counterpoint.

(Reference to the use of the opening idea of the subject as material for an episode will be made later—see p. 124.)

There is a point which should not be passed over before we leave this example. If we look closely, we shall see that it illustrates MELODY as the QUEEN moving freely as she will, and before whom HARMONY the King gracefully gives way. In bar 3 rather amazing things happen.

Ex.166

Obviously the *impulsive* counterpoint of the semiquaver flights has not to be interfered with, even though the subject idea in the other strands might claim priority of consideration. Surely this is *true* counterpoint, melody maintaining her age-long right, going her way free and unimpeded. Doubtless we see here the master at work, not the apprentice. Were such a thing as the above done to-day in an examination it is hoped that the candidate would have discerning examiners; I have reason to think that he would.

A further point having reference to a later or final episode. In our lay-out it was explained that the choice made concerning the material for the first episode was influenced by the possibility and probability of its use in an interchanged form later, generally the third or final episode in the scheme. Now in this fugue the material of the first episode is used again in the final episode and extended somewhat, but the interchange is not very noticeable. The semiquaver figuration remains in the bass and the upper parts do change places, but as they are canonic in character this interchange counts for very little. *Nevertheless we do see the idea of Episode I appearing in an interchanged form with appropriate adjustments as Episode III.* But the student may wonder why Bach did not take more advantage of the interchangeable counterpoint of the first episode and place the running semiquaver strand in the Alto or Soprano. I think there is a reason. In an earlier episode (following the first) covering bars 12-15, there is the same semiquaver figuration which appears in the soprano. The figuration however in this case is in contrariwise movement to that of the first episode (bars 10 and 11). Thus a return of this passage in the bass is refreshing. Let the student also browse over the C♯ Major fugue, Vol. I, No. 3, and compare bars 7-10 and 48-51; also bars 12-14 and 28-30. He will not have wasted his time.

II. Bach's Fugue in E major (Vol. I, No. 9)

The material or idea of the episode is derived from the latter part of the subject continuing itself as the counter-subject,

And in the following quotation can be seen how Bach uses his material └─┘ , in his FIRST episode.
    x

This illustrates sequential repetition of the whole bar figuration x and also slight figure development in bar 3 where the first half-bar of x is sequentially treated in the latter half, while in bar 4 the whole is rounded off and relieved by a downward run. Against all this the Tenor indulges in long suspended notes, and in interchangeable counterpoint. The Bass walks leisurely along in quaver steps also in interchangeable counterpoint. It begins in C♯ minor and also ends in this key, but during its course touches G♯ minor and F♯ minor.

The episode is made by the sequential repetition and development of an idea from the latter part of the subject, *against which two other parts (also sequentially treated) are written in interchangeable counterpoint.*

Further use is made of this episode later. It appears in an interchangeable form in the key of E major, the running semiquavers occupying the middle strand, the suspensions being transferred to the upper one. The quavers remain in the lowest strand, but they are *not an exact repetition* of the first episode. Modification takes place freely. In this Bach teaches us that there is no particular virtue in exact repetition; we see the spirit at work, or perhaps we should say at play. In either case it is true freedom! At every turn we meet with modification. Bach does the very things which the student avoids or fails to do. Perhaps he has been afraid to do such things or having dared has been reprimanded! Here is the episode as it appears later:

III. Bach's Fugue in E♭ major (Vol. I, No. 7)

The material of the episode is clearly the codetta x⌐▭⌐ *which links up the subject with the point of entry of the Answer.* Thus:

Let us see how Bach uses this in the Episode.

The figure  is first of all responded to antiphonally. This goes on throughout bars 7, 8 and 9. In bar 10 the first part of x is repeated sequentially and in the manner of development. A little later in bars 12 to 17 this episode appears again, but in fresh guise. It is a perfect example of an interchange of material written in triple counterpoint. The Bass strand in bars 7 onwards to 11 appears in the Treble in bars 12 onwards to 15 and the other strands are similarly changed over. It should be examined carefully. From bar 15 the episode is extended to 17 in a colourful manner.

This episode is made by a figure being antiphonally used and also developed, the three strands forming interchangeable counterpoint.

IV. Bach's Fugue in D major (Vol. I, No. 5)

Although a four-strand fugue, I mention it here because the points it contains are fundamental, and applicable generally. Cecil Gray[1] says of this fugue:

'The whole piece is so straightforward and simple, so lacking in any deep implications of any kind, that analysis is wholly superfluous. A charming and admirable piece of music, it is one of the most unfugal of fugues ever written, but none the worse for that. The extravagant initial flourish of the subject is the most striking feature of the piece, and dominates it from beginning to end. There is no regular counter-subject but the figure marked with a bracket in the following quotation gives rise to a progression which plays an important role in the various episodes.'

The student should have his fugue book open and follow carefully.

¹ *The Forty-Eight Preludes and Fugues of J. S. Bach* (Oxford University Press).

The first thing we discover is that the above quotation is neither part of the subject nor the counter-subject. It is a short rhapsodic extension of the subject forming a link or codetta between the Answer and the re-appearance of the subject. This illustrates what has already been mentioned, that the codetta may and often does provide material which plays an important part in the weaving of the fugue. Follow to bar 9 where the first episode begins. (There is an unusual point here, for already the subject has appeared in the relative minor without an episode having led to it.) The episode leads from B minor through A major to G major, the sub-dominant key. The extravagant initial flourish of the subject is incorporated into this episode thus:

The *material of this episode* springs from an idea outside the subject, but belonging to the *codetta* connecting the Answer with the second appearance of the subject.

The episode is made by simply treating this idea in sequence, producing . This new result b, is in turn sequentially repeated. This is accompanied by two strands, and *later* we meet it all again freely interchanged in bars 17-19. The semiquaver passage is retained melodically in the bass while the accompanying strands preserve their rhythm , but not their chordal positions (see bars 17, 18, 19 below). This is applied interchangeable counterpoint, the spirit of the law being kept but not the letter.

The student should follow this fugue to the end for he will see how this initial flourish dominates all else.

So far we have seen something of the technique mentioned on page 23 regarding the first episode; sufficient at least to provide food for both thought and practice. But we have not seen all. Dr. C. H. Kitson in his book, *Fugal Construction*, says:

> 'It is tolerably easy to write a grammatical episode. The chief diffi-
> culty lies in preventing it from standing out as a separate section. The
> maintenance of continuity and unity are two essentials of good fugal
> writing. Students generally have no notion how to obtain these results.'

In my experience students generally seem at a loss what to use and how to use it. Often they choose some fragment which does not fit rhythmi-cally with comfort and so works contrary to the idea of continuity. Or, they choose or 'drop on' some idea of their own not deriving from or relevant to material in hand and so contrary to the idea of unity. But we have seen Bach at work, indeed so clearly, that to do as he does seems easy and inevitable. He has shown us the *way*, and we must try to follow. There are many more examples that should be carefully studied.

DOUBLE OR TRIPLE COUNTERPOINT SHOWING INTERCHANGE WITHIN THE
SAME EPISODE

This point of applied technique is mentioned on page 28 in the *Alter-native Lay-out* of an Examination fugue. It has great value and must be given due attention.

I. Bach's Fugue in E minor (Vol. I, No. 10)

This is a two-strand fugue. A moment's reflection will help us to realize how little opportunity for providing potential material for epi-sodes is afforded within the limited bounds of a two-strand exposition. In spite of this I do not think that Bach introduced new material not derived from the exposition. Rather, the clue to the episode (bars 15-19) is to be found in the new counterpoint which he created above the counter-subject in the sixth bar.

This downward scale has character, emphasized by its appearance again in the sequence of the eighth bar. The *spirit* of this lives throughout the episode beginning in the fifteenth bar, and marked *⌐▭▭¬ ⌐▭▭¬.

The episode is simplicity itself, each bar being an interchanged form of the previous one, at a different pitch.

The material of the episode is a new counterpoint created above the latter half of the counter-subject.

The way the episode is made is by adding an accompanying strand to the new counterpoint, and repeating these in the next bar in interchanged form. The two strands are in interchangeable counterpoint.

II. Bach's fugue in G major (Vol. I, No 15)

The following example is not quite such a simple affair. It is not the first episode in the fugue, *but it springs from the codetta* joining the Answer to the second appearance of the subject (bars 9 and 10).

These two bars show not only the strands changing their places, but also the material used in contrary motion.

This is the way the following episode is also made.

It is interchangeable counterpoint with the material itself appearing inverted.

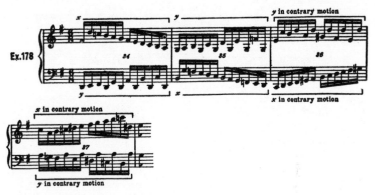

III. Bach's Fugue in B minor (Vol. I, No. 24)

The following episode is more subtle.

The material of the episode is the opening idea of the subject accompanied by two strands forming triple counterpoint.

The episode is made by showing these strands in interchanged positions in successive bars.

The soprano strand in bar 41 is the opening idea of the subject. It appears in bar 42 as the alto strand, and in bar 43 as the Bass strand.

The Bass strand in bar 41 appears in the bass in bar 42, and in bar 43 as the soprano strand.

The Alto strand in bar 41 appears in the soprano in bar 42. In bar 43 it again appears as the Alto strand and is slightly modified. It is worth noting that bar 41 in B minor is sequentially repeated in E minor (bar 42) and also in A major (bar 43).

IV. Bach's Fugue in C minor (Vol. I, No. 2)

What more perfect specimen of interchange within an episode could there be than the following which occurs in this oft-quoted C minor fugue? Is it not a gem?

Ex.180

The material of the episode the student may quickly discover for himself. The way the episode is made speaks for itself. Let him look up Vol. II, No. 13, of which bars 13-16 form another delightful example of this craft.

Such things as these cannot fail to fertilize the musical thought of all who study them.

THE PURPOSES OF EPISODES

Episodes are the means of

(a) Effecting transition from one tonal centre to another.

(b) Creating change, variety, contrast.

(c) Creating colour and maintaining tonal and architectural *balance* in respect of the whole composition.

Let us consider these

(a) Means of *Modulation, transition from one tonal centre to another.*

We see modulation very directly effected in the C minor fugue, Vol. I, No. 2, bars 9-10 constituting the first episode.

Ex.181

The basis of roots rising in fourths (C-F) (Bb-Eb) is one of the simplest and most valuable methods of modulating as it lends itself to sequential workmanship. This shows the idea *applied to a transition from a minor key to its relative major*.

Let us see how this episode can be used later, as Episode III, when, according to our lay-out, it will appear in interchanged form. The transition will be from the *sub-dominant minor* (F minor) to the *tonic minor* (C minor).

How can the material of the first episode from C minor to E flat major be fitted into the third episode from F minor to C minor? A little thought will show the solution to this apparent difficulty. Thus:

Think of the *third* episode as a parallel scheme passing from F minor to its relative major A flat and then by *extension* moving on to C minor.

Harmonic route. F minor-B flat minor, E flat-A flat, extended F minor-G major, to C minor.

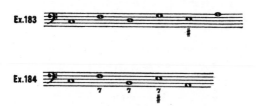

Similarly in the *major key* of C the first episode will move towards A minor and the following harmonic routes suggest themselves

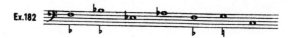

As the middle entries will be in the sub-dominant key F major the third episode will pass from F major to the final section in C major.

Think of this episode as a parallel scheme to the first passing from F major to D minor (balancing C major to A minor) and then *by extension moving on to C major*.

Harmonic route

If in a *shortened* lay-out of a fugue in a major key (C) there were only one set of middle entries in the *relative minor*, the episode would lead to the final section in C major. It can be seen that the Harmonic route just shown (from F major to C major) could be used. The tonic chord of A minor could precede the given harmonic route, and touching upon F major and D minor keys would provide colour.

But although the student should know clearly how to manage his modulation, he must not be content with *one* plan of achieving it. For instance the episode from Fugue in G major, Vol. I, 15, quoted on page 115, Ex. 178, moves from D major to E minor (bars 34-38) and touches upon G major, C major, A minor and then establishes E minor. In the Fugue in D major, Vol. I, 5, the first episode moves from B minor to G major, bars 9 and 10. On its second appearance it is extended and moves from E minor to D major. These cases should be carefully looked up, and the student will doubtless be inquisitive enough to see what Bach does in others.

(b) Means of *Creating change, variety, contrast.*

The episode, by the simple fact of its touching new keys, is a means of change. The new use of potential material residing in the exposition also endows the episode with freshness. But there is another means of creating variety and contrast within an episode, which seems to have escaped notice. I refer to THE MORE SPARING PARTICIPATION OF THE STRANDS DUR- ING EPISODES.

Students often ask 'How many voices should take part in the first episode of a three-strand or four-strand fugue?' They say, 'I know one voice should be dropped, but . . . I never feel certain about all this. . . .'

Such a question and doubt may be answered and cleared by realizing the contrast brought about by a more sparing participation of the strands. In other words, by a *thinning-out* producing a lighter texture.

Now it is obvious that this thinning-out need not indicate *fewer* strands, but it does imply that the strands will be travelling more lightly than in the immediately preceding section. I would suggest that the student should make a study of the following fugues, Vol. I, Nos. 2, 9, 11, 12, 15, 21. These and other excellent examples of this thinning-out will be far more helpful in a practical way than any endeavour to lay down hard and fast rules regarding the number of strands to be used. It is *how* they are used—the circumstance of their use—that matters.

This calls forth a reminder that this thinning-out or pruning must not be regarded as synonymous with any weakening of vitality. Fewer strands do not necessarily indicate anything of this kind. The particular moment of an episode may call for an intensifying of activity such as rounds off the previous working of ideas or contrasts with it; on the other hand a relaxing of activity may be the desired element. The matter is entirely governed by the psychological and artistic demands of the moment as judged by the composer as he directs the expansion of the fugue.

An observation which may easily be missed is that the area of the exposition which involves *all* the strands is only the length of the subject. Thus the weaving process has only just got under way when the episode is reached. Now particularly in three-strand fugues, if the number of strands is reduced at this moment, the effect may not be desirable; not only because of disturbing the texture now under way, but also because the advent of the episode may thus be emphasized. Now, as Dr. Kitson strongly warned the student, the episode should *not* stand out. This would seem to be an explanation of the fact that Bach in his three-strand fugues often keeps all the strands of the exposition at work during the first episode, with modification of some kind as already discussed (texture lightened). It is perhaps worth mentioning that whereas in the exposition activity has been more or less equally distributed among the strands, Bach in the episode often focuses this activity more upon one particular strand, by sequential treatment of an arresting idea. As an example illustrating these several points I will quote from the Fugue in B flat major, Vol. I, No. 21. Others are Vol. I, Nos. 2, 3, 6, 7 to mention just a few.

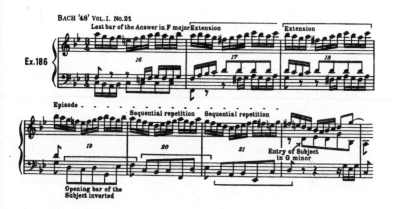

It would be helpful for the student to have his fugue book open. It will be noticed that the episode covering bars 19, 20, 21 drops into two strands. But already Bach has indulged in three-strand writing from bar 9 to bar 19 (by means of a redundant entry of the answer and its extension), so that there has been a good stretch of it; the dropping down to two-strand writing gives welcome change.

Later on from bar 29–34 there is an interchanged version of this episode with a free third strand used appropriately. This is interesting, because although the episode has been preceded by a fair stretch of three-strand writing, yet three-strand writing is continued. But it is *thinned-out*. It will be noted that in bars 33 and 34 the strands revert to their original positions of the first episode.

This is an example of interchange within the same episode:

It should be noted that the figure ⌐___⌐ in the bass of bars 33 and
34 is slightly hidden—it is, in effect

which shows the treble of bar 30 quite clearly.

(c) *Means of creating colour (a 'double-prong' episode) and maintaining
tonal and 'architectural balance' in respect of the whole fugue.*

It is interesting to discover that Bach's technique in Episodical work
did not always confine itself to the sole purpose of transition from one
tonal centre to another. There are cases where an episode, *having arrived
more or less quickly at the new key in which an entry of the subject is expected,*
is *deliberately expanded* from this point. During this digression a series of
modulations is made, after which the subject is announced in the key
which was established before this expansion began its course. (This I call
a 'double-prong' episode; see also paragraph 12, page 127.)

Thus we see Bach using the episode *to add colour* to the fugal design.
No doubt he had a reason for so doing, and we shall see that the key
scheme of the fugue, being a rather limited one, invited it. This type of
episode is by no means uncommon. Now when this kind of thing happens,
another consideration would seem to have been in Bach's mind—the
consideration of balance in a tonal and architectural sense in respect of
the whole fugue. A reference to one or two fugues may help towards an
appreciation of these points. Let the student turn to the *Fugue in E major*,
Vol. I, No. 9. A broad analysis shows:

A^1. Bars 1-10 consisting of exposition and counter-exposition in the
Tonic and Dominant keys.

B. Bars 11-18 consisting of an episode, deliberately expanded, and an entry in the relative minor key.

A^2. Bars 19-29 consisting of the final section in Tonic and Dominant keys with a touch of the sub-dominant key.

The design is a ternary one and in order to maintain an architectural balance Bach makes the sections of about equal length. As there is only one entry of the subject in the middle section B, Bach lengthened this portion by deliberate expansion of the episode preceding that entry.

The *main tonal centre of section B* is the relative minor key. Thus we may fairly say that the key scheme is as yet limited. This gave Bach the opportunity to add colour by means of digression through the keys of G♯ minor and F♯ minor, re-establishing C♯ minor in bar 16 in which the subject enters.

But there is more than this to be noted. Bach wrote the extended portion of the first episode (bars 13-16) in double counterpoint with free quaver bass. He uses this, showing an interchanged form of it, in the final section A^2. Although sections A^1 and A^2 *balance each other in length and tonality*, yet A^2 is not a replica of A^1. The counter exposition of section A^1 is replaced in A^2 by the appearance in interchanged form of the extended portion of the first episode, during which further colour is created by touching the sub-dominant key A major. The whole is rounded off by the entry of the subject in tonic key at bar 25, and appropriately prolonged.

Is not this a masterpiece of design?

The *Fugue in E flat*, Vol. I, No. 7, is an interesting parallel to the E major fugue just examined. There is an exposition (in which occurs codetta material), followed by a sequential and imitative episode leading to a redundant entry of the answer. This corresponds to the exposition and counter exposition in the E major fugue. Then a short episode (bar $12\frac{1}{2}$-14) at which point the dominant chord of the relative minor key is reached and leads one to expect the entry of the subject—but instead, the episode is deliberately expanded (bars 14-$17\frac{1}{2}$) and after colourful harmony returns to the relative minor key, at which point the subject makes its appearance. This corresponds to the middle section of the E major fugue. There is, however, in this E flat fugue an answer in G minor in this section. After this we pass through another episode and reach the final section. The answer occurs first, then the codetta, then the subject (bar 29). Quite a good reference is then made to the extended portion of the episode in bars 14-$17\frac{1}{2}$ after which occurs the final appearance of the theme. This is modified and extended and winds up the fugue. Thus again we see Bach using this type of episode for the purposes of colour and architectural balance.

All this reveals to us more of Bach's perspicacity and versatility. But of these two qualities there is far more to be discovered in the '48' than can be even mentioned within the limits of this book. I am only too painfully aware that this short work merely touches the fringe of Bach's technique and thought as revealed in the '48' alone.

The 'double prong' episode serves a fine purpose, particularly in a somewhat short lay-out as in I, 9 and I, 21 and may well be incorporated in the full lay-out for an examination fugue (containing three episodes). Further reference to this will be made later in Chapter XI.

Now let us briefly consider, with our fugue book open,

FOUR-STRAND FUGUES

It has been said, earlier in this book, that after the exposition Bach's fugues unfold in a bewildering variety of ways; moreover, that each fugue was a particular work, created, not according to a set plan, but from the inherent possibilities and power of the subject.

We have already seen that three-strand fugues do not generally resort *much* to two-strand work in order to afford contrast, although two-strand effect has its place. Contrast came more by way of varying the texture rather than the number of the strands. Further we have noted that Bach did not usually interfere with a texture that had only just got under way in the final section of the exposition. No doubt this was all related to the *balance* of the complete fugue.

But we may wonder how he controls these matters in his four-strand fugues. We can be certain that he applies the same *principles* and the same sure judgment as in the three-strand fugues. It will probably startle us to find that out of the opening twenty-eight bars of a four-strand fugue—itself completed in the thirty-fifth bar—only four bars exhibit four-strand work! That is what happens in the *A flat major fugue, Vol. 1, No. 17*. The last seven bars maintain four-strand writing, but nowhere else in the fugue are there two consecutive bars of it. To be exact there are four isolated bars studded at different points acting as punctuation marks one might say. Look at the whole fugue, and it will be conceded that the end justifies the means. Bach knew how the initial material should be used to reach the peak of its power. What a *tour de force* are those final four-strand bars! If the four-strand work in bars 10 and 18 for example is examined it convinces us that its busy nature is too much to be kept up for long. In Bach's plan it affords contrast to the more prevalent three-strand work, and this may have been his design.

As this book is not an investigation into fugue as 'composition' it is not essential to examine each of the remaining four-strand fugues. The student should do his own spade-work and look carefully at Vol. I, Nos.

14, 16, 18, 20, 23, 24. Brief comments upon one or two of these should however be made, which may help us in our deductions.

Fugue in B minor, Vol. I, No. 24

The exposition is *extended* by a delightful imitative display upon the figure in the last bar of the counter-subject during which four strands are maintained. Clearly, it may be said that as an appreciable stretch of four-strand writing has been in progress (bars 13-18), the resort to three-strand writing in the ensuing episode is well-timed.

Thus in a four-strand fugue whose subject is of fair length as in this case, the idea of extending the four-strand work of the exposition might well be borne in mind as it justifies three-strand work in the episode.

This fugue in $\frac{4}{4}$ time is seventy-six bars in length. The subject is three bars long. Apart from the four bars comprising the final section of the exposition and its extension, and the last six bars of the fugue there is practically no other four-strand work except for a half-bar or so here and there. Apparently such places serve the purpose of punctuation. It is a case rather parallel to the A flat fugue, Vol. I, No. 17, except that the subject is three bars long and not one.

Fugue in B major, Vol. I, No. 23

This fugue is thirty-four bars long, and contains only eleven bars of four-strand work. Six of them occur about midway (bars 12-17) and four at the end, with another bar 21-22.

The placing of this four-strand writing suggests a broad half-way punctuation, indicating binary balance. The subject is two bars in length and invites counterpoint of an active kind. As in Vol. I, No. 17 and Vol. I, No. 24, this may have influenced Bach's choice as to the amount of continuous four-strand work. The lay-out of the fugue is quite different from Vol. I, No. 24. The exposition is remarkable; it has only half a bar of four-strand writing. As the final strand enters in the Bass, the Tenor becomes silent. This three-strand writing is prolonged throughout the episode which leads to a redundant entry at which point four-strand writing really begins. Having got under way it is continued throughout the following episode. This episode is, in a subtle way, an interchanged version of the previous one (in three strands) with a fourth strand added— bars $13\frac{1}{2}$, 14, 15. This fourth strand is free.

In four-strand fugues it might strike us that it is the shortish subjects which invite a redundant entry. At any rate I, 18 and I, 23 give rise to such a thought. But I, 16 and I, 17 just make fun of it. Bach's opening out of the material in these pairs of fugues should be examined. In I, 18 and I, 23 where there *is* redundant entry, there is little or no codetta. In I, 16 and I, 17 where there is *no* redundant entry there is ample use of codetta material. The two methods really serve the same basic purpose of providing a good preamble in the home keys. (Incidentally the pair I, 14 and I, 20 might be compared.)

These fugues are, like all the '48', examples of the art of composition in fugue. To the student preparing for an examination test they show that *balance* was a guiding factor in Bach's mind. It was behind all the varied *placing* of four-strand work, and gave it purpose as our scrutiny has shown. This is particularly clear in the B minor Fugue, I, 24, which might almost be looked upon as a three-strand fugue, with four-strand writing reserved for special effect.

As a broad principle for examination fugue it would be well to bear in mind that when four-strand writing has just got under way in the exposition, it should not be blindly cut off. Sensible judgment with regard to the situation will prevent the student from making the mistake of using either a too long or too short stretch of it. Generally speaking the three-strand episode will be in prospect; to lead into this, an artistically relevant extension of the exposition may be invited.

Whereas in three-strand fugues Bach *generally* maintains three-strand work and does not resort to fewer parts, in four-strand fugues he does *not* generally maintain four-strand work, and resorts much to three-strand writing.

The student will find that many things have a way of arising and compelling his attention as he is at work on episodes; but he should now be able to consider them, at least in some degree, in the manner and spirit of Bach. As he becomes more and more engrossed in the study of Bach's writings he will realize how great is Bach's mind and how sure his judgment. For Bach laid hold on deep and permanent principles which crown his work with coveted qualities, namely, *authority* and *persuasive power*. These principles are not confined to the art of music. They are common to all the Arts and are demonstrated in the masterpieces of all schools of painting. The Fugues of Bach have as their closest kin the pictures of the old masters. Books about these things may be attractive and helpful to the student, but it is to the music and the paintings he must go in order to learn and to know.

CONCERNING THE USE OF THE OPENING IDEA OF A SUBJECT, AS MATERIAL FOR AN EPISODE

This moment may not be an inappropriate one at which to refer to a matter of important significance. Students have often asked if the opening idea of a fugue subject might be used as material for an episode. My reply has been to the effect that Bach does use such material in making episodes, but apparently in certain circumstances only.

These circumstances appear to be when *stretto* is not a feature of the fugal treatment.

The force of this is apparent because an episode of an imitative or canonic character is suggestive of stretto—is of the same species of technique—and would spoil the freshness of the effect at a later stage of the fugue.

Bach's awareness of this is evident in the following fugues of the '48', in which episodes occur involving imitative work based upon the opening idea of the subject and suggestive of stretto. But Bach makes no use of the stretto device later.

> Fugue in C minor, Vol. I, No. 2.
> Fugue in E flat major, Vol. I, No. 7.
> Fugue in F sharp major, Vol. I, No. 13.
> Fugue in B minor, Vol. I, No. 24.

The following fugues should be mentioned too. In the B flat fugue, Vol. I, No. 21, an episode occurs in which the opening idea of the subject is repeated sequentially in *the same strand* (bars 19, 20, 21). Against this idea which is in quavers, is a continuous semiquaver movement in the upper strand. This may attract the ear more than does the quaver figure and so hide the use of this opening idea of the subject. Be that as it may, Bach in the later part of the fugue makes only a very mild use of stretto device, two entries at two bars distance. In this case stretto could not be called a feature of the treatment.

In the D major fugue, Vol. I, No. 5, is an interesting use of the opening of the subject. The initial flourish comes into play not only in the episodes, but throughout the fugue (see page 112). It is clear enough why there is no example of stretto.

The student therefore might well decide that if he makes stretto a feature of his treatment, he will avoid using the opening idea of the subject in episodes; or if he uses this opening idea as episodical material he will *not* make stretto a feature of his fugal treatment.

A summing-up of this chapter

1. The purpose of the exposition, from the point of view of *BALANCE* tonally and architecturally, is to provide a good stretch of music in the home keys.

Among Bach's schemes for achieving this are the following:

(a) An exposition followed immediately by a main episode. In this case it is likely that good codetta-spaces are brought into play, lengthening the exposition and providing potential episodical material.

(b) An exposition followed by a shortish episode or link, leading to a redundant entry or possibly entries of the subject or answer. After which the first main episode occurs (and this may be a restatement, in some varied fashion of the shortish episode, possibly showing it in an interchanged version and extended).

In this case the plan of the exposition does not require codetta spaces as a feature, as it provides a sufficiently long stretch in the home keys without them.

Minor-key fugues seem *naturally* to invite codetta space (particularly between answer and second appearance of the subject) far more than do major-key fugues. These latter seem to associate themselves more with the redundant entry or counter exposition. These observations do not apply invariably, but at least they are of interest

These two schemes (a) and (b) should be borne in mind for examination work particularly when the modified and shortened lay-out is chosen. The first scheme (a) is recommended as being more general, particularly when the full lay-out is followed; for the codetta-space work need not be drawn out. It can be adjusted or perhaps dispensed with entirely.

2. A three-strand or four-strand texture that has just got under way as the exposition closes should not be disturbed or broken off at the episode. The point to realize is that the appropriate moment for a decided change has not been reached, although the *textural character* of the episode will vary from that of the exposition.

3. In three-strand fugues the continuance of three-strand writing throughout the first episode commends itself.

4. In four-strand fugues it would be wise as a rule to extend somewhat the four-strand writing just under way, and then fall into three-strand work for the episode. (Not one of the schemes for four-strand fugues which we have scrutinized is likely to be followed as *a whole*, in an examination fugue.)

5. Double or triple counterpoint is a general feature of the episode, even when a figure is pursued in one part and draws attention to itself.

6. The episode often affords change from the expositional texture by thinning-out. Bach was fond of focusing the activity in an episode mainly upon one voice which sequentially repeats and perhaps develops some figure. The other voices chat responsively one to the other. The *effect* might well be the chatter of *one* voice (as Vol. I, No. 2, illustrates) showing the idea of thinning-out behind it all.

7. If an episode has the same number of strands as the exposition preceding it, we may expect the next section of the fugue to show change in this respect. After the thinning-out process, relief or change may happen

by restoring the more compact writing, or by reducing the number of strands and creating work of new character.

8. Episodes always spring from some relevant material of the exposition. Such material should be wisely chosen.

9. Although Bach's episodes at times modulate through a series of keys and return to their starting-point thus providing change by *means of colour*, this is not generally contemplated in our lay-out for the examination fugue. In this, the episodes will as a rule bridge over from one main key centre to another (but see paragraph 12 below).

10. Interchangeable material in the first episode lends itself to further use. It may appear, in an interchanged form, as a later episode in the fugue.

11. Even within the same episode an inversion of material may be shown. This type of episode should be borne in mind when a modified lay-out of the fugue is being adopted, and in which two episodes instead of three are used.

12. The 'double-prong' episode is one which seems to have two sections (which *may* make use of the same material). The first section effects the modulation and arrives at the new key early. The second section makes a deliberate excursion from that point, passing through a cycle of keys, and returns to the original new one at a point where the subject makes its entry. It readily yields itself to re-statement in interchanged or modified form later in the fugue as another episode. It may be applied in some modified lay-out of our examination fugue.

Chapter Eight

THE FIRST MIDDLE-ENTRY SECTION

This section of the fugue follows upon the first episode. Although it may consist of only one entry of the theme, it presents points of interest.

First we will consider

THE MANNER OF ENTRY OF THE SUBJECT

(a) The entry should coincide with the cadence establishing the key so that a new interest springs up at that moment.

(b) It has been shown that not necessarily fewer voices take part in the first episode. This, particularly in three-strand fugues, may often mean that the voice introducing this middle-entry of the theme, does so *without breaking its own continuity*. In other words it has had no period of rest.

(In four-strand fugues this is not so likely to happen for the reason that the episode has probably not maintained four strands, one of them having rested for a space. This particular strand would introduce the subject in the new key.)

(c) Now when a voice of the episode leads without break into the subject it is possible that it may cause some modification of the opening of the subject. Here are some instances:

Ex.192 iv. Vol. I. No. 11 Subject / Modification

Ex.193 v. Vol. II. No. 19 Subject / Modification

Thus we see the opening note (or notes)

i. Displaced by two short notes which slightly alter the contour of the melody.

ii. Shortened, reduced in length to one half and one quarter of the original.

iii. Omitted, or as some may say, displaced.

iv. Displaced by an ornamentation of the outline.

v. Preceded by an additional note.

These examples suffice to indicate that the opening of the subject yields to the artistic impulse of the moment. Bach regarded the region round about the opening note as one of elasticity, not rigidity. The student, having seen *why* Bach made these modifications, will have no need to refer to rules.

Secondly we will consider

HOW THE OTHER STRANDS ARE OCCUPIED DURING THIS MIDDLE-ENTRY SECTION

THREE-STRAND FUGUES

Case A. Showing the subject accompanied by the two counter-subjects of the exposition in an interchanged version
Fugue in C minor, Vol. I, No. 2.

We find the first middle entry in bars 11 and 12, the subject being in the relative major key of E flat. Along with the subject are the two counter-subjects (see bars 7 and 8) presented in a new relationship, showing triple counterpoint with a slight modification. We note that the figure which has persisted throughout the episode slightly overlaps the new entry in E flat and gracefully ceases activity.

We cannot fail to notice that the three-strand work of the exposition and first episode continues throughout this first middle entry. We are inclined to ask whether a change from this would not have been appropriate after the episode. We must remember that this fugue is a fine example of composition in fugue, expression by means of fugue and that Bach was fully aware of dangers and master of them too. This fugue is only thirty-one bars long and its very character—quickish, delicate, crisp, whimsical—

safeguards it against monotony; the necessity for reducing the number of strands at any point does not arise.

Case B. Showing the subject accompanied by one counter-subject, the third strand resting

Fugue in C sharp major, Vol. I, No. 3.

We find, in bar 14 and onwards, the subject accompanied by the original counter-subject only, while the third strand rests (compare bars $2\frac{1}{2}$ to $4\frac{1}{2}$). This is interesting because the exposition and first episode have been employing three strands and so falling into two strands undoubtedly affords contrast for a few bars. The fugue is fifty-five bars long, much longer than the C minor fugue just considered. Bearing this in mind, and the busy texture of the exposition and first episode, we realize that Bach obviously considered the question of relief and planned his two-strand work with sure judgment. Further proof of this will be forthcoming if the student will study the remainder of the fugue with an eye to this particular matter (see bars 35 to 43).

The voice which rested after bar 14 during this middle entry will be seen to enter as an imitative strand in the following episode. This is worth noting; students are inclined to think that after a voice has been silent it should and must next appear announcing the theme of the fugue.

Let us now glance at

Fugue in E flat major, Vol. I, No. 7, which is somewhat similar to the C sharp major fugue just considered, *in lay-out* up to this point. It is thirty-seven bars long and the character of the subject is quite akin to the C sharp major one. As it is much shorter, we should not expect as much two-strand relief. We find this to be the case, for only five bars are in two-strand writing (bars $15\frac{1}{2}$–$20\frac{1}{2}$). An observation concerning the *placing* of this two-strand relief patch may be worth mentioning. It occurs in the very centre of the design which is as follows: 15 bars three-strand work, 5 bars two-strand, 17 bars three-strand. From this angle of thought it seems clear that Bach had his wits about him. Reference[1] to this power of structural thinking in the mind of Bach has already been made in the previous chapter.

The middle entry at bar $17\frac{1}{2}$ shows the subject in the relative minor

[1] The student should look through the whole '48'—it will be a delight, and he will be amply rewarded. The maintenance of interest and provision of variety compel the composer to keep an alert mind regarding the problems of structure, plan, balance. He cannot ignore them with impunity. Bach in the D sharp minor fugue, Vol. I, No. 8, which is eighty-seven bars long, maintains interest in spite of keeping the three strands engaged the whole time except for an occasional rest of a beat or so. How does he achieve this? Is not our curiosity aroused to action?

key (C minor) accompanied by the original counter-subject (compare bars 3-4) while the third voice rests, exactly as in the C sharp major fugue. The subject and counter-subject are extended for one and a half bars, by using an interchanged and modified version of the codetta beginning at bar 4½. Then an answer appears introduced by the third strand which has been resting. Thus Bach uses two entries of the theme in this middle-entry section. The reason for so doing is clear enough if the lay-out of the whole fugue be examined. It concerns *balance*.

A point to note is that the figure which persisted throughout the episode ceases activity abruptly when the theme enters at bar 17½. The theme for the moment takes over the activity. We shall see more of this kind of thing.

Case C. Showing the subject accompanied by a free strand, or strands

A careful scrutiny of the E major fugue, Vol. I, No. 9, will bring to light a very interesting stroke of technique. There is an exposition ending with three-strand writing which is maintained throughout the first episode. It is not until after the middle-entry section has begun at bar 16½ that Bach falls into two-strand writing. As is quite a favourite way of his, Bach throughout the preceding episode has concentrated upon a figure in the soprano part. It reaches a climax at the beginning of bar 16, at which point—after rising and rising—the figure descends (see a ▔▔▔▔).

Ex.194

For the moment its activity subsides, yielding pride of place to the subject reappearing in the Alto. But note that the activity is handed over to the subject, which is so constructed that the activity of the episode is merely transferred to it, similar to the case of the E flat major fugue above. In passing on this activity the soprano part continues and becomes a *new counterpoint* against the theme as shown - - - - - -.

Ex.195

But this figure (a) cascading from the episodical climax evidently appealed to Bach's imagination for he weaves it into the soprano strand running against the newly-introduced subject, as shown at (a) bar 17½. Moreover so pleased is he about it that he repeats it in sequence against the extension of the subject (in sequence) in bar 18. He thus creates a passage containing freshness; it runs naturally into and overlaps the entry of the subject in bar 19.

Ex.196

This figure catches and maintains the spirit of the episode out of which it springs though it does not appear quite as a direct development of it in the ordinary sense. It provides a *new background* to the fugal theme, *gives it a new setting*, and *therein lies the value of this stroke of technique*. Altogether it presents us with an attractive illustration of the use of what we have called 'potential material'. This fugue subject has a regular counter-sub-ject, which the above technique causes to be put aside for the nonce; but not without compensation.

Now the above shows the subject in the middle-entry section accom-panied by material which maintains the *spirit* of the preceding episode, rather than by material which shows development of the germinal figure of that episode. But one can easily imagine the subject of this middle-entry section being accompanied by the germinal figure itself for some distance. Bach does this in some measure in this E major fugue where the episodical germ continues after the entry of the subject in the counter-exposition.

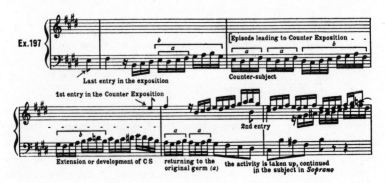

Ex.197

We saw a similar thing in the C minor fugue, Vol. I, No. 2, but it was referred to by saying that 'the figure of the episode slightly overlaps the subject and gracefully ceases activity'.

The above shows how this procedure can be of value when a second entry of the theme is used in this first middle-entry section. A second entry may or may not be in stretto. If the subject is short then stretto is not likely. At or about the point of the second entry of the theme the figure would *gradually close,* or *yield to some other idea,* or even return to the germ from which it began. Often the activity is passed on to the subject as is shown in the case we have quoted, and this is the thing to note.

A fuller illustration of this point of technique (which presents the theme in new surroundings) is to be seen in

Fugue in A major, Vol. II, No. 19.

The original counter-subject is not regular and does not recur. The eight semiquavers ⌊ ᵃ ⌋ which close the subject lend themselves to considerable use as the basis of codetta and episode. The figure ⌊ ᵇ ⌋ has significance too.

There is a redundant answer shown below, followed by an **episode**

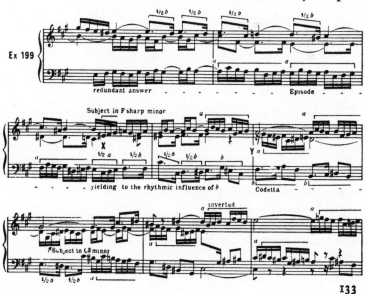

built upon the eight semiquavers ⌐•⌐ again. You will see that the episodical germ ⌐•⌐ subsides when the subject enters, and yields to the less active germ ⌐ᵇ⌐. It should be observed that as the episode subsides, its activity is as it were handed over to the subject entering in F sharp minor at X. This subject ends at Y, and so far it is all somewhat parallel to the course of events traced in the E major fugue, Vol. I, No. 9, except that before the answer appears in C sharp minor there is a codetta of a bar's length. It is from Y that the progress of things should be most closely followed. The codetta concerns itself with the final group of semiquavers ⌐•⌐ belonging to the end of the subject. It occurs in the Alto, then Soprano, after which the answer in C sharp minor appears. But notice the subtleness of the *opening* figure of the subject here, which in effect is so closely akin to ⌐•⌐ that it appears as carrying on that figure. This ⌐•⌐ appears in the Bass, in the Alto, in the Soprano in an inverted form and again in the Alto as an extension of the subject which closes at this point.

Thus we have, both at X and at the bar after Y, presentations of the theme of the fugue in *new surroundings* by the persistence of a figure springing from the previous episode in some manner. The bars quoted are a masterpiece of craftsmanship and musicianship.

By pursuing this fugue a little farther, continuing from the point above, we see still another new setting of the subject. The soprano strand all derives from ⌐•⌐. This further illustrates the value of this point of technique.

Ex 200

Were this book an unrestricted excursion among the highways and byways of Bach's '48' I should now turn my steps in the direction of the fugue in F sharp minor, Vol. II, No. 14; but we must now consider the behaviour of voices taking part during

The first Middle-entry section in Four-strand Fugues.

FOUR-STRAND FUGUES

We will keep our investigations parallel to those of the three-strand fugues under cases A, B, C and see if the procedure in four-strand fugues is similar.

Cases A and B. Showing the subject accompanied

A by its *three* counter-subjects (as shown in the last entry in the exposition) *in an interchanged version.* This corresponds to the *two* interchangeable counter-subjects in three-strand fugue.

B by *two* of its three interchangeable counter-subjects, with the fourth strand resting. This corresponds to the *one* counter-subject and the third strand resting in the three-strand fugue.

Fugue in F minor, Vol. I, No. 12. This fugue provides examples of both the above cases. Let us open our book at this fugue. We shall first encounter case B and then case A a little later.

The exposition ends at the first beat of bar 16. Bars 13-16 are in quadruple counterpoint, that is, each part is capable of taking its place as the bass.

(*Case B.*) A three-strand episode based upon ♫♪♫♪ occurring after the end of the subject (at bar 16) leads to a *redundant entry of the answer* (in bar 18) which is accompanied by the 1st and 2nd counter-subjects, while the 4th strand rests. This is Case B.

(*Case A.*) This is followed by an episode (an interchange of the previous one) leading to a redundant entry of the subject (F minor) which is accompanied by 1st, 2nd and 3rd counter-subjects interchanged. This is Case A.

These parallel considerations serve to show the same deep principles at work in Bach's mind and applied to both three- and four-strand fugue.

But let us pursue this closely-knit fugue a little further and see what other things come in our path. Continuing from the redundant entry of the subject ending at bar 30, there is an episode leading to the appearance of the theme in the relative major, A flat, the first entry of the subject in this Middle-entry section.

Cases parallel to C. The subject is here accompanied by the first counter-subject and two free parts, the last-mentioned being in the Tenor and Bass. So that this corresponds to Case C where, in a three-part fugue, this middle entry shows the theme accompanied by one or two free parts: in addition the theme is accompanied also by the first counter-subject. But there is more than this, for as we shall see, the Tenor part is a free continuation of the material of the preceding episode, overlapping quite two-thirds of the subject, to the first beat of bar 36, and indeed similar in technique to the cases C in three-part fugue.

If we look carefully into the preceding episode from bar 30 we shall find that it springs from the link which joins the subject to its counter-subject or continuation (bar 4 ♫♪♫♪). At bar 30 this figure has the last note lengthened ♫♪♫♩ ♪ and the two lowest voices converse together upon it. When the subject enters in A flat major at bar 34, Bach carries this episodical idea forward in the Tenor part for about two bars thereby adding to the interest of the texture which already contains the subject and its first counter-subject, besides which there is a free part in the Bass. It will be seen that the episodical figure ♪♫♪ ♩ ♪ is not slavishly adhered to, but that its spirit is maintained; by thus regarding the spirit rather than the letter of that figure, artistic results were come by which otherwise would or might have been lost.

Ex. 201

Following this, however, is an episode which links up with an entry of the *answer* in E flat major, and it is during this answer that we meet with a close parallel to the three-part fugue, *for here the theme is accompanied by three free parts.* Here too the spirit of the episodical idea, already conversed upon and developed, is maintained either by one voice or another, not merely throughout a good part of the theme, but throughout its entire length. The excerpt below shows part of the episode from bar 39 and the complete subject following it.

Ex. 202

The brackets indicate how Bach used and maintained the **germinal** ideas of the episode, combining with the subject *in spirit rather than to the letter*. He was not concerned here about *exactness* in the repetitions of the fragments which, dovetailed together, became the accompanying texture to the main theme. Exactness, for its own sake, had no place in Bach's mind; it must serve and yield to the greater impulse which in music must be unfettered by the laws of the Medes and Persians.

Apropos of this it may be pointed out incidentally that Bach modifies his fugue subject at *. He did not hesitate to vary even a fugue subject! Such an occurrence is by no means rare with him, for there are more of them hiding among the leaves of the '48'. Now what was Bach doing in all these instances? He certainly never thought of being clever or displaying skill of any kind. We know well enough how *his* art conceals art. Surely the answer is that he was absorbed in music-making, expressing thought and feeling in music, which was the playground of his imagination. That being so how could the letter restrain the spirit? No wonder he adorned those intimate melodies of the Choral Preludes with such tender beauty.

Continuing our study, another example—this time from the charming Fugue in G minor, I, 16—may afford instruction. Although simpler in character than the one from the F minor fugue, it *shows the subject combining with its original counter-subject, a free part, and also a part which catches the eye as a stretto. This last-mentioned is the fresh point to note*. In my opinion, it seems clear that although it cannot be regarded seriously as a stretto yet it does occupy the place of an entry in the sub-mediant major key of E flat and thus affords new colour to the scheme.

Let us examine the few bars in which this happens.

It is well to note an important fact, that the original counter-subject does not commence until after the fourth note of the subject; it can be taken for granted that this space will be well used by Bach, and it will be seen how he allows the germ of the counter-subject ♪♩♪♩♪ to

extend over it, thus making good account of the stroke of technique to which the attention of the student has already been directed. Besides this there are two free parts going on although one of them, the Alto, stops on the second crotchet of bar 17, but only to bring in the stretto or rather pseudo-stretto of the subject in E flat later in the bar.

Note carefully that the subject in B flat earlier in bar 17 continues its full length, closing with an inverted perfect cadence in B flat major, so that evidently the E flat subject entry is quite a secondary consideration. (In real stretto[1] the opening note or notes of the voice making the stretto entry are not altered to 'fit in' with the voice already leading; nor is any note during the progress of the leading voice altered to oblige the voice making the stretto entry.) The adjustment in the pseudo-stretto entry serves a good purpose for in bar 18 the theme follows its true course and a dash of E flat major colour is provided.

This may seem a somewhat subtle touch, but it should not lead the student into the practice of altering the stretto-entry of a subject to suit his convenience (or inconvenience). He must determine clearly between true stretto and pseudo-stretto for both have their use; in our lay-out the place for the latter is in the final section of the fugue.

This chapter could be extended, but it has provided examples and ideas relating to this portion of the fugue, and shown how the material of a link or episode can, by overlapping the next entry of the subject, add interest to the fugue and be a technical asset.

A SUMMARY OF THIS CHAPTER

1. The opening notes of a subject may be modified, particularly when the subject is led into *without break* by a voice taking part in the preceding episode. The region about the beginning of the answer Bach regarded as an elastic and not a rigid area, yielding to the artistic impulse of the moment.

2. *In Three-part Fugues* the types of treatment of the middle-entry section following upon three-strand work in exposition and first episode are:

(a) *Three-strand work* showing the subject accompanied by its two counter-subjects in some interchanged version.

(b) *Two-strand work* showing the subject accompanied by its original counter-subject. (Note: this leads into an episode in which the voice which has been resting takes up an imitative strand.)

(c) *Two-strand work* showing the subject accompanied by its original

[1] See also ch. x which concerns Stretti.

counter-subject. (Note: this is extended somewhat when the voice which has been resting enters with the *answer*, thus making two entries of the theme in this section.)

(d) *Two-strand work* showing the subject accompanied by a free part which is a new growth from the preceding episodical material. It is as though the episodical idea expands beyond its own sphere, overlaps the new entry of the subject and develops against it. This type of procedure offers attractive possibilities.

3. *In Four-part Fugues* the types of treatment are more or less parallel to those in three-part fugues.

(a) *Four-strand work* (following a three-strand episode) showing the subject accompanied by its three counter-subjects of the exposition, in some interchanged version.

(b) *Three-strand work* (following a three-strand episode) showing the subject accompanied by two of its counter-subjects in some interchanged version while the fourth voice rests.

(c) *Four-strand work* (following a three-strand episode) showing the subject accompanied by its *first counter-subject* and *two free parts*. Of these free parts one is an extension or free continuation of the material of the preceding episode.

(d) Four-strand work showing the subject accompanied by *three free strands*, two of which toy with an idea from the preceding episode while the remaining free strand indulges in a figure which has appeared prominently in earlier episodes.

Altogether this chapter has brought to mind a wealth of fugal technique. The student cannot be too strongly urged, when considering this section of the fugue, to study carefully how Bach *places* his three- and four-strand work (in four-strand fugue) and his two-and three- strand work (in three-strand fugue) *having regard to the whole composition*. There is never anything haphazard about this placing. Rather does it reveal Bach's critical sense of balance, proportion and musical effectiveness. It shows consummate skill hidden in the apparently simple and inevitable.

Chapter Nine

THE SECOND EPISODE

Canonic and imitative work

In this chapter examples of both canonic and imitative work in episodes will be considered, as the technique is much the same. Imitative writing may be regarded as a free use of the canonic idea. An imitative episode well framed and carried out has a musical virtue no less commendable than the canonic episode.

The student who condemns canon is usually one who is uneasy about it. He is not the master of it, and is uncertain about the outcome of any attempt he may make. If he has thought about his difficulty at all he considers himself weak in counterpoint or imagines this to be so. In my experience it is not so often that he is weak contrapuntally as insufficiently alert harmonically. Counterpoint is the flight of melodic tracery between one harmony and another. The working of canon depends largely upon being able to grasp in a flash all the harmonic possibilities offered by a particular note at a particular point. For this leads to the choice of a suitable continuation of the antecedent; it provides the harmonies between which melodic thought can spin its tracery. If the wrong harmony is chosen, it prejudices all that follows.

The type of canonic writing used in fugue has freedom in respect of quality of melodic interval. It is not at all the straight-jacket idea of canon that is essential. Canonic writing, strict as to melodic interval, does occur in Bach, but only when it serves the highest purpose. Sir Percy Buck, in his *Unfigured Harmony*, says that strict canon in its stereotyped forms is probably a thing of the past as far as composition is concerned. He gives a simple working of a canon at the fifth below, and the consequent part adjusts its intervals as occasion demands. For example, at bar 10 an accidental is introduced in the consequent which was not in the antecedent. This, says Sir Percy, is always allowable and is one of the main methods of reaching a new key, especially in canons at the octave. This is, no doubt, instruction based upon Bach's works. In Bach's 'Goldberg Variations', Variation III, is a canon at the unison carried out strictly. Variation XXIV is a canon at the octave, and with the exception of one note, G sharp in bar 12, answered by G natural in bar 14, this is strict. But that single

140

alteration, which is indeed vitally important, gives us Bach's mind about the matter. The other variations showing canon at 3rd, 6th and 7th are all adjustable, free. The student should examine these as well as the Two-part Inventions[1] which contain delightful examples such as Nos. 2 and 8. He will see Bach at work in these, and if wise, will work with him by copying out these examples and pondering over them. They will provide him with technical training of an attractive kind. The student may be reminded that Bach learned much by copying out the works of other composers.

As far as fugue is concerned, canonic work need not continue for long. Even in a lengthy episode, such as occurs in the fugue in D minor, Vol. II, No. 6, canonic work may be pursued for only *part* of the way; in other words, Bach uses it with discretion. The late Dr. Charles Wood's compositions abound in examples of canon. We often see that there is adjustment of *some kind* after a short spell. A book[2] of *Twelve Vocal Canons* by Dr. Wood illustrates this, as do such things as his Evening Service in A flat. Immediately artistic purpose has been achieved and there is danger of artificiality, the canonic idea is prolonged no further—it is not carried on for the sake of it. I mention the works of Dr. Charles Wood to the student because he is a modern composer who made canon a very live force of expression. A study of his works will teach the student a great deal about the ways and means of canonic writing.

We will now consider canonic work as applied by Bach in the '48'. The student will not fail to notice that it falls under three main heads, namely:

(a) Sequential Canon, dove-tailing canon.
(b) Continuous Canon.
(c) Applied canonic work, that is, free imitative writing.

Fugue in D minor, Vol. II, No. 6 (example of sequential canon, and also free imitative writing).

Bars 19 and 20 are as follows:

Ex.204

---

[1] The Two- and Three-part Inventions contain the finest examples of double and triple counterpoint. They are a gold mine for any student in search of technique and knowledge.
[2] Published by the Year Book Press, Ltd.

The full idea of the canonic figure is shown in the Alto bar 19 ‿‿‿‿‿. This full idea is seen again in bar 20, but although this could have been shown in all voices Bach chose to play with a shortened version of it shown ⌐▬▬▬. Thus we see clearly a canon at the octave after the strict manner, between Bass, Soprano, as indicated by ⌐▬▬▬. It is what may be called a *Sequential, dove-tailing canon*. There is a continuous process of overlapping. It also follows a course of modulation by a series of dominant-tonic harmonies. It derives from the opening figure of the subject, inverted. If we look ahead to bars 21, 22, 23 we shall see that the canonic work begun in bar 19 *does not continue for long*. At bar 21 the episode breaks away from strict canon and pursues a course on lines which are however *akin* to canon, that is *free imitation* of a figure by various voices. Students are inclined to carry out their canonic episodes, continuing in canon to the bitter end, no matter what the cost. This particular example shows us Bach's wisdom. Here are bars 21, 22, 23, for they illustrate the difference between canon and imitation:

These are imitations and free imitations too of (a) ⌐▬▬▬. These bars should be compared with 7, 8, 9 of which they are a modified restatement.

The imitations are not exact mathematical affairs. They remind us of the nave of some old abbey, of which no two pillars are quite alike in contour, or adorned by just the same tracery. Therein lies their charm.

Bach's work abounds in this free imitative writing, and it always runs along easily and simply. Its very fluency hides the skill behind it. The following examples show what Bach could do with the simplest of material, reminding us too, that he was always ready to do something new and attractive.

Fugue in E major, Vol. II, No. 9 (examples of flowing phrases forming prolonged or continuous canon).

Here are the opening bars of the fugue showing subject and counter-subject.

A counter-exposition closes at bar 12 (^{2}), but the theme immediately links on to itself the *regular* counter-subject the latter part of which appears in augmentation (the quavers becoming crotchets and so on). This regular C.S. is traced in the Alto at half a bar's distance, then again in Bass and Tenor. The canon might be regarded as being at the fifth above (or fourth below), but *not strict* as regards interval. What good purpose would strictness in this respect serve? Rather, what artistic purpose would it not cripple? This is an example of canon because the theme overlaps the next entrant and pursues its full course. In fact, it is a specimen of '*stretto maestrale*' in which a phrase in its full length is repeated in canon through-

out all the strands. Such a thing is usually connected with the final section of the fugue where stretto is often a feature, the theme treated being the fugue subject. One does not expect to meet this in a student's examination work, for it is not a common occurrence even in Bach.

Later in this fugue, beginning at bar 23, is another episode based upon canon. Two voices, Soprano and Alto, enter in canon at one beat's distance and continue for two bars, when the Bass and Tenor enter similarly. Thus we have *two-part* canon, with two free parts accompanying. Let the student study also the *harmony* of these bars.

But we must continue for a few more bars, as we merge into another section of this episode also in canon and quite parallel to the bars 23-26 just examined.

It will be seen that in bar 30 the subject is introduced in the Alto as the Bass clings to the little theme of the canon; this kind of thing continues, thus presenting the theme in a new background, to which attention was drawn in the preceding chapter.

In connexion with the above examples of canon I would wish to draw the student's mind to the *material* from which the two canons are woven. Look at these two themes carefully.

It has been mentioned already that episodes should spring from material 'exposed' in the exposition of the fugue, or from material concerned with the exposition indirectly. Can it be said that the two themes under consideration are relevant material? Let us first examine the canonic theme beginning in bar 23.

Is it not the fugue subject itself, subtly disguised?

And cannot the same be said of the second canonic theme? It is, in fact, the theme in 'diminution'.

Incidentally I think it should be pointed out that throughout the course of this fugue there is much *stretto*. That being so it is clear why Bach disguised the subject when using it in these canonic episodes. (It will be remembered, as has been stated, that when Bach indulged in stretto as a *feature* of a fugue, he avoided the use of the opening of the subject as material for an episode of an imitative character.)

Bach shows us that metamorphosis of themes was practised long before the nineteenth century.

Fugue in F major, Vol. II, No. 11 showing imitative devices in a lengthy episode.

The student should have his fugue book open.

The fourth and fifth bars of the subject provide material for much varied episodical work of imitative character.

The codetta between bars 9 and 14 shows us the first treatment of a figure arising from this and becoming

The episode between bars 17 and 21 (in which a *redundant answer begins*) shows

This might be condensed into the following two-part construction

Bach makes an artistic thing of this by placing it as he does. An important example of *how to extend a subject* occurs from bar 24 to 28. Look at the Bass prolonging itself cleverly.

This extension of the subject is the *first section* of a long episode stretching from bar 24-52. The *second section* from 29-37 is concerned with the episodical material which has already appeared from bar 17-21. The *third section* concerns itself with the material of the codetta 9-14, but treated with closer imitation or free canon.

In bar 44 the Bass singles out the final bars of the theme and by a series of sequential sweeps reaches bar 52 in which the subject enters once more.

These examples show us how Bach worked with his material, always relevant and apparently perfectly natural and simple. Although an Examination fugue is not likely to call for lengthy episodes nevertheless we have seen how Bach created such and did not confine himself to one idea.

Fugue in E flat, Vol. II, No. 7, showing the *theme disguised,* and used sequentially in two-part canon at two bars distance with a third accompanying voice.

When pointed out, this canonical writing is transparently clear and altogether creates a most attractive episode. The *dove-tailing* is not so obvious, being at a distance of two bars, and one is apt to overlook this in performance.

The theme of this canon is the fugue subject disguised, similar to the examples already quoted. Compare the following quotations, the second of which is the metamorphosis of the first.

It is interesting to note how the four-quaver group (a) steals in upon the ear at bar 43 for the first time. It adds a fascinating and welcome touch of liveliness which Bach seemed loth to dispense with (as we have noted earlier in this book), so he introduced it in his decoration of the theme which immediately follows treated in canon, and it served a *double* purpose!

Now Bach in this fugue makes stretto *quite a feature*, and yet uses his fugal theme in his canonic episode; but he disguises his theme, hides it from the listener, and so does not depart from the effectiveness of his stretti.

Fugue in B minor, Vol. II, No. 24, showing sequential, dove-tailing canon, in two parts *founded upon two small fragments*—one from the subject, the other from the counter-subject, linked together forming a new but quite natural musical thought.

Here are the subject and part of the counter-subject.

After the exposition is an episode leading to a redundant answer at bar 26. Let us examine this episode.

It is a simple canon in two parts, without any third voice accompanying. Upon what relevant material is it built? It is founded upon material occurring at different points in the subject and counter-subject. Thus, bar 6 of the subject flows along quite placidly ♪♫♫♫. In bar 9 the counter-subject has an arresting idea |♫♩·♫|♪. Together these two form an excellent and quite natural idea which is relevant material. My reason for drawing attention to this particular point is that students seem to be at a loss when choosing material for their episodical work. Frequently they ruin the unity and coherence of their fugue by building episodes upon some irrelevant idea. They introduce a *wrong kind of diversity*, contrary to the very character of fugue which is *diversity within unity*. The episodes should be built upon material *within* the bounds of affinity as expressed in the exposition or counter-exposition.

Chapter Ten

THE SECOND MIDDLE-ENTRY SECTION

The use of Stretto

The attention of the student has been drawn to observations concerning the opening notes, or all, of the fugue subject as material for a canonic or imitative episode. So far it has been pointed out that

i. Bach appears to use the subject in this manner, only when Stretto is not a feature of the fugue.

ii. Bach, on occasion, makes the above statement (i) look at fault, for he *does* use the theme as material for a canonic episode, although indulging in stretto as a strong feature of the fugue. Such are Fugues, Vol. II, No. 7 and No. 9. But he *disguises the fugal* theme in these instances. Obviously he is respecting his general procedure as suggested above (i), see pages 143 and 146.

But there is another observation concerning this matter. It is that

There are fugues in which Bach has quite clearly given prime thought to the stretto device, in all its variety. These cases take us a step beyond even the fugues mentioned under (ii). (Bach's mind, when writing the fugues 7 and 9 of Vol. II, although *mainly* focused upon stretto, did not have *all* the episodes involving the subject material. And moreover the subjects were used in *disguised* form.) The great C major fugue, the first of the '48', is perhaps an unique case. The whole composition is a virtuoso study of stretto, to the exclusion of all else. Even episodes are dispensed with, and quite reasonably enough too, for Bach did not need them. But the '48' afford us examples which, while not disregarding the place of episodes in their scheme of design, yet forcibly suggest that it was Bach's intention to make Stretto a *supreme* feature. In fact, Bach's structure and use of the episodes in these cases definitely reveal this to be his purpose. It is clear that he based them upon the fugal theme, and this in no sort of disguise. He so created them as to provide new varieties of stretto, additional to those occurring in non-episodical periods. He fearlessly fused them into the design. Bach in achieving this peculiarly unified texture turns completely away from the avoidance of the fugal theme in episodes towards the fullest use of it. His boldness of thought and design is convincing; it truly serves the purpose of expression and is carried out by unerring skill and judgment. Such fugues as Vol. I, No. 8, Vol. II, Nos. 2, 5 and 22, illustrate in varying degree stretto as the *supreme* feature of the technique. I would ask the student to look up the following examples of Bach's craftsmanship:

Vol. I, No. 8, Fugue in E flat minor (three-strand fugue).

Bars 19-21. *Two* entries of subject at two beats' distance.

Bars 52, 53. *Three* entries at one beat's distance.

Bars 54, 55. *Three* entries of *subject inverted*, at one beat's distance.

Bars 61-64. *Two* entries at two beats' distance. The subject on its second entry is in augmentation.

Vol. II, No. 2, Fugue in C minor (four-strand fugue).

Bars 14, 15. Subject *in full* followed at a half-beat's distance by subject in full, and in augmentation. This followed by subject (not in augmentation) but *inverted*, at three and a half beats' distance.

Bars 16, 17, 18. *Four* entries at *two* beats' distance.

Bar 23 (in final section of the fugue). *Two* entries at one beat's distance.

Vol. II, No. 5, Fugue in D major (showing treatment of four-strand stretto).

Bars 21, 22. *Two* entries in full at *one bar's* distance and a third entry at half a bar's distance.

Bars 27, 28. *Two* entries in full at one beat's distance.

Bar 33. *Three* entries in full at one beat's distance.

Bars 44, 45. *Four* entries in full at one beat's distance (stretto maestrale as already mentioned, page 143).

This fugue contains much that is instructive to us, and I cannot refrain from quoting bars 21-28 referred to above. These bars are a *complete middle-entry section*, beginning in the relative minor key (B minor) and involving the answer in F sharp minor. Let us examine it.

The first observation concerns the beginning of this section. It does *not* start after a perfect cadence which has brought all voices to a close, as is the case for instance in bar 27. The entry in the tenor is accompanied by some other voice continuing or winding up. There is overlapping. The overlapping notes in the soprano (a) play an important role throughout the fugue. They figure a good deal in this middle-entry section.

The answer in the Soprano of bar 22 is a true response and runs its full length, ending with a tierce de picardie.

In bar 22 the Alto enters, and in order to oblige the harmonic circumstance E sharp appears. Evidently Bach had no compunction about this. The rest of the subject is normal.

In bar 24, the section could end, but it is extended by means of the relevant figure (a) ⌐⎯⎯⌐, leading to an appropriate moment for another entry of the answer in F sharp minor, without any stretto being involved. This answer itself is extended to close with a perfect cadence in bar 27[*].

This middle-entry section shows us the kind of freedom, musical ease which Bach enjoyed. The stretto entries are not at regular distances, but at *suitable* distances which *assist* musical expression, not hinder it. Bach alters a note of the fugal theme, because by doing so he is serving a higher purpose than he would do by preserving the *exact* restatement of the theme. This stretto work is relieved for a little while in bar 24, and the subject in bar 25 enters with all the more clarity and significance, winding up the whole section. It is a model of musical sense from which we should learn a good deal, and improve our own power of judgment and confidence.

Vol. II, No. 22, Fugue in B flat minor (four-strand fugue).

Bar 27 Stretto. Two entries in full at *one beat's* distance at the interval of *major 7th*.

Bar 67. *Two entries in full* at *one beat's* distance at the interval of *minor 9th*. The subject used in *inverted form*.

Bar 88. The subject in full, followed by *subject in inverted* form *in full* at *one beat's* distance.

Bar 96. The *subject in 6ths* (and in latter part in 3rds) followed by subject in *inverted form in 3rds throughout*, at one beat's distance.

The student will here see Bach's amazing skill, particularly from bar 96 onwards.

This kind of work is hardly expected to be displayed in an examination fugue, but it shows what possibilities can arise on occasion.

⠀ . ⠀ . ⠀ . ⠀ . ⠀ . ⠀ . ⠀ .

Now let us turn to more normal examples occurring in fugues in which stretto is not a stressed feature of the design. We will see how these stretto sections begin, of what they consist in the way of material, particularly the accompanying strand or strands. How sections of a fugue *dove-tail* into the design is of great importance; none the less so is how the strands behave, what use is made of relevant potential material, subservient to the stretto weaving.

Vol. I, No. 6, Fugue in D minor, showing Two-strand stretto with an accompanying part.

Here, in bar 17, we see in the soprano strand the figure (a) ⌐‾‾‾⌐ from the counter-subject used as accompaniment to the subject in the bass. It also carries on the spirit of the preceding episodical bar, and is again seen at (a) ⌐‾‾‾⌐ in bar 18 doing similar service as the second strand of the stretto enters. Appropriate movement is thus kept up. In bar 19 note how the Bass strand, having run the full length of the subject, takes up the figure (a) ⌐___⌐ while the theme is going on in the Alto strand. For the moment the soprano sinks into the background.

Thus we see:

The first entry of the theme, not starting off alone as though starting a new section, but *overlapped* by relevant material arising from or in the spirit of the preceding episode. Also we see the first theme, its course completed, taking up the counter-subject against the newly entered second strand of the stretto. The first theme in this case has run its full length; but it might not have been possible for it to do this, so we should say that having pursued its course *as far as possible* this strand takes up the counter-subject against the recently entered theme. *This is the guidance we gather from examining this stretto section.*

It is well to note that immediately a point of repose, that is a feeling of cadence, is reached, a new interest springs up, or continuity is preserved by means of a part pursuing its course *beyond the cadence*. The student should observe that accompanying strands do not aimlessly plod along. This is of first importance.

Let us follow this fugue a little further, continuing from bar 21.

This shows a two-strand stretto without any third strand accompanying. The theme, on its second appearance at a bar's distance, is in *contrary motion*. Then at bar 23 the leading strand itself has the theme in contrary motion whilst the soprano picks up the (a) ⌐──── motive from the counter-subject. It is important to note this.

At bar 25 this stretto section merges into a short episode or link of two bars, illustrating how the weaving goes on and the design is gradually displayed.

Fugue in F major, Vol. I, No. 11, showing three-strand stretto.

This fugue provides interesting examples of stretto. From bars 24–31 is a *two-strand* stretto with an accompanying part. The student should study it in addition to those quoted from the D minor fugue above, especially observing the accompanying part, linking up with the previous bars, and how this stretto section *merges into* the following episodical one at bar 31. Surely the earnest student will not be at a loss as to what material to use and how to use it, after browsing over these examples from Bach. His self-criticism will be all the better too, refusing to allow incoherent bits and loose ends. Let us follow this fugue a little further.

My purpose in quoting these bars is a manifold one, but chiefly do I wish to impress upon the student the absence of awkward 'joining places'. Here we see the ending of an episode (bar 35) leading apparently *naturally* into the stretto section; there is no awkwardness. The figure (a) ⌒⌒⌒ maintains the spirit of the episode; Bach never used inappropriate material.

Another thing I feel these bars show clearly is the way Bach could wind-up a section. Students are frequently in a great hurry to do this and rob their work of any grace at such places. Look how Bach works to a close from bars 43 to 46; and again, quite differently, from bars 53-56. Note too that although a full close is established at both these points (bars 46 and 56), there is no sense of a stop. Without hesitation the weaving goes on. Again this is achieved with perfect smoothness and as though it could not be otherwise. This fugue is one of the most transparent to be found and one which should have no small influence upon the student in his examination studies.

The Pedal occurring about half-way through the fugue (bars 36-40) will be a surprise to many. This is a matter to which reference will be made later.

The treatment of four-strand stretto has been well illustrated on page 151, **Ex. 227**, by quotation from the Fugue in D major, Vol. II, No. 5.

THE SECOND MIDDLE-ENTRY SECTION

A summing-up of this Chapter

1. Examples of the use of stretto as the supreme feature of a fugue are referred to in Fugues, Vol. I, No. 8 (three strand), Vol. II, No. 2 (four strand), Vol. II, No. 5 (four strand), Vol. II, No. 22 (four strand). *These show to what lengths of imagination and intensity the stretto idea may go; always serving a musical end.*

2. In all cases quoted, the student should observe the way in which Bach links up one section with another. This is always done with such an ease and smoothness that one is apt to overlook the craftsmanship and musicianship behind it.

   (a) At times the previous section overlaps the stretto beginning.

   (b) At others there is a full close after which a new start has to be made (but without drawing attention to itself or in any way being an awkward moment). The student will note that a strand may begin the activity before the leading stretto strand appears, or the activity may begin by the immediate appearance of the stretto-strand.

3. The accompanying strands (if any) should be carefully examined. They are a common source of trouble to the student and show his poverty of thought. He is apt to shirk these most important *little* things (which make all the difference). Let him refer to Vol. II, No. 5 (quoted on page 151, Ex. 227), Vol I, No. 6 (pages 152, 153, Exs. 229 and 230), for there he will see how to use the relevant material.

4. The following are illustrated:

   Two-strand stretto with an accompanying part, Ex. 229, page 152.
   Two-strand stretto without accompanying part, Ex. 230, page 153.
   Three-strand stretto—dove-tailing together, Ex. 231, page 154.
   Four-strand stretto (all parts fully occupied), Ex. 227, page 151.

Chapter Eleven

THE THIRD EPISODE

Having reference to an earlier episode. Parallelism, balance and modification of treatment and key schemes. Single-prong and double-prong episodes

In the lay-out of our examination fugue, mention was made of the fact that the first episode should be written in double or triple Counterpoint, because of its probable use later on in an interchanged form. In the alternative lay-out two episodes only are planned for, the first of which, it was suggested, should show double or triple counterpoint with an interchanged version of it, within its own ground (because it would not be made use of later). In our three-episode fugue, obviously the third episode is a suitable place for an interchanged form of the first episode.

The student would be wise to read once again Chapter VII and refresh his memory about first episodes. Much in that chapter will be referred to here. Among the fugues we shall discuss are the following:

Vol. I, Nos. 2, 3, 7, 9, 21.
Vol. II, Nos. 13, 17, 19, 24.

Some have single-prong episodes—that is, built upon one idea and treatment. Others have double-prong episodes—that is, built upon one idea, but making two definite sections showing different treatment, or upon two ideas, each having its own section. With regard to the later use of the first episode it will not be difficult to discover parallel treatment, which though often involving modification creates a balance as it were. Parallelism in the key schemes of the two episodes may not, at first sight, always appear to exist. Nevertheless I think we shall find that Bach is as clear-headed about this as we have found him to be about other things concerning fugue.

We shall find that Bach frequently constructs an early episode showing interchange within its own ground. I would emphasize the fact that he did not hesitate to use this episode later on in some varied form. I mention this lest the student should think that he must not show an interchange in an episode which he intends to use later.

My method of endeavouring to help the student is to group together fugues which seem to illustrate this or that aspect and so create a definite impression upon his mind.

A. *Fugue in C minor, Vol. I, No. 2*

Here we see the first episode, passing from C minor to its relative
Major E flat, *re-stated later almost exactly*. I say *almost*, because although
this later episode modulates from C minor to E flat as did the first, yet there
is a difference, in that the two upper parts are interchanged. As was mentioned on page 109, this interchange is not very noticeable in effect.
The later episode thus affords a good parallel to the first so far, but *then
continues a little further* until it reaches again the key of its starting-point
C minor. Such an exact restatement as this is not likely to occur in our
examination fugue. Why Bach used it is talked about in Chapter VII,
page 107. It is all decidedly convincing.

B. *Fugue in E flat, Vol. I, No. 7*

Here we meet with the first episode in triple counterpoint used, not
once, but twice later in the fugue. *The second episode is an interchanged version of the first: but the key process is not quite a parallel.* The first episode
begins in B flat major, passes through E flat major, A flat major, F
minor and then E flat when a redundant entry of the Answer appears.

THE THIRD EPISODE

The second episode beginning in E flat major does not follow a parallel succession of keys. (But let it be observed that this is due entirely to subtle chromatic adjustment of intervals without any interference with the sequence, as far as bar 15, after which Bach indulges his fancy to good purpose.)

The first episode, which might be regarded as starting in E flat major, passes through A flat major and F minor thus providing a little colour and returns to E flat. This is after the style of episode produced in the double-prong cases, in which the second prong starts from the desired key and finally returns to it after an excursion through various keys providing colour.

But the second episode *moves* from E flat major to C minor, and a study of this example should prove to the student that no stereotyped succession of chords need be followed in achieving it.

There is a *third appearance* of this episodical material from bars 30⁸-34, passing from B flat major to E flat major as did the first episode. Bach keeps the more active voice in the bass strand and this is an exact repetition of the first episode except for one note; D flat in bar 9 does not occur as D flat in bar 32. The other two strands however are quite changed in

outline but not in character—Bach preserves the spirit, as always; but how he loved variation! So this third episode teaches us that it is not essential for an earlier episode to be *exactly* repeated but rather that its spirit is to be maintained. Bach knew how to use to advantage both diatonic and modulating sequence; this is to be seen constantly.

C. *Fugue in A flat major, Vol. II, No.* 17

The first episode shows triple counterpoint interchanged within its own ground, and when it occurs later there is *perfect parallelism with regard to key relationship.* It is a single-prong episode.

Broadly outlined

Episode I extends from bar 10^1-13^1 and moves from E flat major to D flat major.

The first part, bars 10^1-11^8, is in triple counterpoint, modulating from E flat to A flat major.

The second part, bars 11^8-13^1, shows an interchange and modulates from A flat to D flat major.

(Being extended a half-bar the key of A flat is established when the theme enters, a redundant appearance, at 13^8.)

A later Episode extends from bar 27^8-30^8 and moves from C minor to B flat minor *which corresponds to the move from E flat major to D flat major in the first episode.*

The first part, bars 27^8-29^1, resembles bars 10^1-11^8, and modulates from C minor to F minor.

The second part, bars 29^1-30^8, resembles bars 11^8-13^1, showing an interchange, and modulates from F minor to B flat minor.

(This is extended by further repetition, 30^8-32^1, from B flat minor to E flat minor.)

Ex. 236

Ex.236a

later episode

C minor . . . . to F minor, . . F minor to . .

. . . Bb minor, . Bb minor to . . . . Eb minor

In the later episode we see the rich results of interchanges, giving three entirely new effects.

The study of these examples should be of great value. They show as clearly as one could wish an interchangeable and modulating episode, transplanted to a later part of the fugue. A new series of keys—minor instead of major—is set up but entirely of similar relationship as in the original. One should not overlook 'extensions' which carry forward an episode to the desired point; they are most important.

Another fugue which furnishes exact parallelism in key relationship, when the first episode appears later, is the one in

C sharp major, Vol. I, No. 3.

Let the student look at the first episode of this fugue which joins the exposition to a redundant answer. It begins at bar 7 and consists of sequential repetitions of this bar until bar 10 is reached. Starting in C sharp major it modulates to G sharp major. Now turn to the last episode from bar 48³ to 51³. Here we see a transposition, but with slight

Ex.237

First episode:-

Ex.237a

appearing later

Variation of interval

variation as to quality of interval, of the first episode, and it follows a parallel course moving from F sharp major to C sharp major. Although in triple counterpoint, there is no interchange of strands.

This slight variation as to quality of interval is well worth noting. We have already seen it and we shall come across it again. In the first episode, the second bar creates no modulation, but a quaintish sequential effect; whereas the slight alteration in bar 50 creates a touch of D sharp minor.

There is another pair of episodes in this fugue showing perfect parallelism in modulation and triple counterpoint later interchanged. We cannot examine too many examples of this kind of craftsmanship, and here again we shall see slight modification in bar 30 (compared with 13).

later, showing interchange:—

Fugue in A major, Vol. II, No. 19 (single-prong episode)

This example shows an exact parallelism in modulation with triple counterpoint, but only the two upper parts exchange places. It is similar in construction to the episode in the C minor fugue, Vol. I, No. 2, where too the running semiquaver figure appears in the bass strand in both episodes. A point of particular interest which should be duly observed by the student, is the *extension of the episode* on its second appearance. Attention to such extension, which serves the purpose of reaching the desired key in an appropriate manner, has already been emphasized.

Note that the redundant Answer ends in bar 8, beginning of 3rd beat and that the episode is built upon the last half-bar of this, sequentially repeated. The accompanying strands also move in sequence. It is worth noting also that, although this redundant answer is in E major, Bach carefully avoids the expected perfect cadence by deliberately using* D natural instead of D sharp. (This kind of thing has been mentioned earlier in this book, see Ex. 134 page 92.) Now let us turn to a later appearance of this material transposed. The above episode moves from E major to F sharp minor; in its new place it modulates from A major to B minor, thus being parallel.

later episode

Ex.239a

Ending of Subject in A major

(a) in contrary motion,

Entry of Subject in D major

Extending the episode to . . . D major

The extension of the episode is interesting, because at this point Bach's quick mind switches the motive (a) into contrary movement. Another matter which will not escape observation is the entry of the subject in D major. Here Bach does not hesitate to lead in the theme by an additional semiquaver (C sharp), with musicianly purpose. Who would condemn him?

Fugue in F sharp major, Vol. II, No. 13

Here we meet another single-prong episode, bars 13–20, written in triple counterpoint and showing an interchange within its own ground: bars 13–16. It is then extended by playing with the first bar of the episode. This idea occurs in the several strands, but is somewhat hidden. The modulation scheme, leaving the tonic key of F sharp behind, moves through D sharp minor, G sharp minor, C sharp major, F sharp major. These keys move up a fourth each time. The same will be noticed in the later episode which moves through G sharp minor, C sharp major, F sharp major, B major. The C sharp major is really C sharp minor ending with the major third. The student should examine the two episodes carefully. He will discover adjustments, and much from which to learn.

Fugue in B minor, Vol. II, No. 24, single-prong episodes

The two episodes quoted below, simple enough in themselves, show how Bach could adapt material to his purpose. The first episode is in triple counterpoint; the two upper parts are canonic in character, and these exchange places in the later episode. As in other cases already quoted, the active bass-strand retains its place in the later episode. But although there is sequential parallelism, yet there is also tonal adjustment, as comparison of bars 32–35, 87–90, reveals.

These two episodes have what one might term, *diatonic subtleties*. For instance—in the first episode, Bach, starting from F sharp minor, is steering towards D major; but he avoids touching A major by the use of the G natural in bar 34. Thus he creates a half-close rather than a full close in A. But in the second episode Bach does not show a parallel behaviour, for he creates a full close here, where he had half-close in Episode 1. Of course this might be accounted for by the fact that he was not steering towards G major at bar 91, as the parallel to the key of D at bar 36. From bar 91 Bach begins his coda, or winding up of the fugue,

Ex.241

which is an interesting piece of workmanship. It passes quickly through A minor and E minor before finally settling down in the home key of B minor.

We have met similar subtleties already—see pages 158 and 161—and no doubt there are many others of like nature from which we may learn.

D. Under this section, I am placing *two examples of double-prong episodes*. It will be recalled that the characteristic point of a double-prong episode is that the second prong returns to the key from which it started, because already in the early part of the episode—the first prong—the desired key has been reached. In a word the episode has two prongs, or two divisions, and in the second division the purpose is to add new *key-colour*, besides at the same time serving to create architectural balance.

Fugue in E major, Vol. I, No. 9

Reference to the episodes in this fugue has already been made on pages 109 and 110. Let us add other observations. In the later episode it will be noticed that only the second prong of the first episode recurs. The episodes are alike in that they return to the key from which they started, C sharp minor and E major respectively. They begin in each instance at bar 13^1 and 22^1 and the semiquaver strand follows a parallel course for two and a half bars—to 15^3 and 24^3. From this point slight variation of outline takes place; and it is interesting to follow and compare the two. At any rate at bar 24^3 Bach breaks away from the first episode 15^3, and continues the last half-bar in sequence, leading to the C.S. in bar 25^3 which uses the identical figure. It is just such a spot as this that the student should think over for a while. Let him ask himself the question 'What should *I* have done at bar 24^3?' It brings to mind Sir Percy Buck who once said to me, 'It's easy to grouse at Beethoven, but how many could carry on if they suddenly found the next page were missing?'

The modulation scheme in these cases does not quite balance.

The first episode beginning in C sharp minor touches G sharp minor and F sharp minor and then returns to C sharp minor. The second episode begins in E major, touches A major and then re-establishes E major. Obviously too there will be the necessary adjustments, by which is meant that sequences will not be reproduced exact as to interval, but will be varied to serve Bach's purpose. This is really the point to emphasize, that in the parallel restatement of an episode even of this double-prong derivation—returning to the key in which it began—adjustments, little subtleties, freely abound which serve the musical purpose. There is no slavish exact reproduction. On the contrary, within the limits of maintaining the spirit, the situation invites the full inventive imagination of the composer.

The two episodes are here again displayed.

Fugue in B flat major, Vol. I, No. 21

In this fugue too we see Bach using the *second division of a double-prong episode as the substance of a later episode, showing an interchange of its double counterpoint.* By means of its first prong, the first episode beginning at bar 16 has reached the desired key of G minor at bar 19. This done, the second prong extends the episode as far as bar 22^1, where it is still in G minor and where the subject makes its entry as expected.

Thus in the second episode we look for a restatement of the bars 19-22. We recognize this from bar $30-33^1$. But let us look closely at this parallel restatement. Something has turned this second episode away from its key of C minor, in which it should still be at bar 33^1, were it an exact parallel to the first episode. What has happened to bring this about? Nothing more than little adjustments—which the eye misses so easily and the ear accepts no less readily—which in sequential work can be skilfully employed to bring about the desire of the composer. So Bach, having strayed purposely to G minor, returns to the starting key of C minor, by extending this later episode for two bars more (up to 35^1). At least let us say this, for the moment; actually there is more to follow. During these two bars of extension we see him, aware of the danger of overdoing repetition, transferring the semiquaver movement to the Soprano strand. Evidence of his musical gumption is always turning up.

If we compare the semiquaver strand in these two episodes we shall see how Bach, all along the line, did not bother about exact reproduction as regards quality of interval in the second episode. How simple a matter it was to divert the key path away from C minor towards G minor at bar 32! The student should so grasp all this, that he may acquire ease and confidence in making artistic use of it in his own work.

THE THIRD EPISODE

A rather interesting thing about this second episode—being a restatement of the second prong of the earlier episode—is that it maintains the tonality of the previous entry instead of the next expected entry! In other words, as the episode begins in C minor we should look for an announcement of the subject in that key to follow on. But the C minor entry occurred *before* this episode! And what does Bach do? At bar 35 he introduces a modified version of the subject starting from C minor, which serves to lead into the desired entry in the sub-dominant key of E flat major. The *balance* of the whole fugue, resulting from all that goes to make the composition, is satisfying, and worth more than a passing glance.

Although this chapter could be extended considerably, yet it is hoped that the examples dealt with suffice to show how Bach handled his material. Clear-minded musicianship was always the inspiring and fearless power which guided his dexterous technique.

Chapter Twelve

THE FINAL SECTION

It has been truly said that the composer's most severe test is the *ending* of a movement. The power to carry a thing to a right and convincing conclusion is indeed an enviable one, no matter whether the thing concerned be a symphony or a fugue. The recapitulation, the gathering together and tying of the threads, the farewell to the adventure—call it what we may—this, accomplished so that it pleases and delights the mind, is a thing 'well and truly' done.

The final sections in the '48' are as varied as the other phases in these fugues. They are affected by considerations of architectural balance, both of material and tonality; no less also by considerations of textural balance giving satisfaction to the weaving habit of mind. The richest texture, representing the fullness of contrapuntal thought, should be creative of the climax in sound and therefore coincident with it. It should give a sense of cumulative strength. This climax may be achieved as late as the final chord, or earlier. In the latter instance some peroration will carry the work to the point of repose. But no matter how Bach brings us to the last sound of all, he satisfies our musical and logical mind. This closing period of the fugue *must* give the mind—through the ear—entire satisfaction. In relation to all that has gone before, it must be the true conclusion; it must complete the design. One might say that it must tell us unmistakably that the 'casting-off place' has been reached and the loom can be stopped.

St. Thomas Aquinas wrote, 'The *beautiful* thing is that which, being seen, pleases.' The late Eric Gill added, 'And when we say the beautiful is that which being seen pleases, let us take it that it is the *mind* which is pleased.' I like to think that such thoughts may also refer to music, and that we may say with regard to it:

'The beautiful is that which being *heard* pleases and let us take it that it is the *mind* which is pleased.'

Every new period or span in the unfolding of a composition must successfully come through this test. It must be 'pleasing to the mind'. This means not only must the period be pleasing of itself, but also in its relation to the whole. In no section of a work is this standard more difficult to attain than in the final one.

Let us now turn again to Bach.

Such items as:

> Stretti.
> Interchange of the Counterpoint of the exposition.
> Pedal points.
> Augmentation, etc.
> Added thirds, etc.
> Contrary-wise movement.
> Bravura passages.
> Alteration of the subject.
> Pauses.

could all be studied in detail. But this cannot and need not be done here. We must be content with a few of these items and see what Bach can teach us about them.

PEDAL-POINTS

Students are inclined to assume that at least one pedal-point must occur in every fugue, no matter what number of strands is involved—3, 4 or more. Also they seem to think that the dominant pedal most certainly should be present; rarely do they think of the tonic pedal. Further, students are apt to think that a Fugue without a pedal-point at all just simply is *not* a fugue! So it may be somewhat surprising to discover that only about one fugue out of every four in the '48' indulges in pedal-point. (The Preludes, by the way, are quite another matter in this respect.) Again, students often seem in doubt as to whether the pedal note itself should or should not be regarded as a real part or strand.

Let us consider Pedal-points as they occur in the '48'.

(The student should have his fugue book open.)

Vol. I, No. 1 (4 strand).

Has a *dominant* pedal for one bar some distance from the end.

Has a *tonic* pedal for the last four bars, which are really a coda or peroration.

They are restricted to four strands. No additional voices are used. The pedal note counts as a strand.

Vol. I, No. 2 (3 strand).

Has no dominant pedal.

Has a tonic pedal for the last two and a half bars forming the coda.

They are *not restricted* to three strands, but the added notes serve the purpose of harmonic effect, not part-writing.

Vol. I, No. 14 (4 strand).

Has a *dominant pedal* for one and a half bars near the end; it *remains* in four strands.

Vol I, No. 15 (3 strand).

Has a *tonic* pedal for the last four bars which form a coda. The pedal is slightly elaborated. These bars are *not restricted* to three strands.

Vol. I, No. 18 (4 strand).

Has a short tonic pedal of one bar in the dominant key near the end. It *remains* in four strands.

Vol. I, No. 20 (4 strand).

Has a *tonic-pedal* of four and a half bars at the end forming a fine peroration. It does *not restrict itself to four strands*. In fact, as written, the player could not sustain the pedal note—it is outside the possible technique, and needs the *organ* pedal. The effect of this pedal note must soon have been lost on the harpsichord which had little sustaining power.

Vol. I, No. 24 (4 strand).

Has a *short dominant pedal* during the ante-penultimate bar. It is *restricted to four strands*. The last two beats of the penultimate bar are also over a *dominant pedal*, but here there are *five strands in all*, creating fullness of effect.

Vol. II, No. 3 (3 strand).

Has a *dominant pedal* for two bars, beginning in the eighth bar from the end. It is *restricted to three strands*. At the fourth bar from the end is another dominant pedal (slightly decorated), *but not restricted to three parts*. The final two and a half bars are over a *tonic pedal*, which at first maintains three strands, but ends with four.

Vol. II, No. 10 (3 strand).

The long *dominant pedal* of nearly eight bars maintains three strands only. The final bar has four strands. The *pedal is decorated*.

Vol. II, No. 11 (3 strand).

There are two examples of pedals in the latter half of the fugue bars 61–65, 76–82, but not at the end. They are restricted to three strands.

Vol. II, No. 16 (4 strand).

Has an *inverted tonic pedal* for two bars near the end. Restricted to four-strand work.

170

Vol. II, No. 18 (3 strand).

Midway through the fugue (bars 93-95) is a *dominant* pedal. It is restricted to three-strand work.

This is similar to:

Vol. I, No. 11 (3 strand).

which also has a dominant pedal for five bars (in the relative minor key) in the middle of the fugue. It is restricted to three-strand work. An analysis of these leads to the following conclusions:

1. In four-strand fugues, *dominant pedals remained in four-strand writing*. In one case only was this not adhered to. Even then it was at the final cadence (I, 24) and obviously for harmonic fullness.

2. In four-strand fugues, *tonic pedals* were sometimes restricted and sometimes not restricted to four-strand writing. It is clear however that Bach did *not* restrict himself whenever his purpose called for more strands; when harmonic fullness was desired.

3. In three-strand fugues, the *dominant pedals* remained in three-strand writing, except in one case of the final bar.

4. In three-strand fugues, the *tonic pedals* were generally not restricted.

Thus we may reasonably sum up by saying that:

Dominant pedals usually restrict themselves to the normal number of strands.

Tonic pedals show no restriction if the purpose demands it.

This is obviously most likely in a three-strand fugue.

An observation that may help us in benefiting from this study of pedals is that *generally the tonic pedal is in the nature of a coda or peroration, where liberty would be expected.* Pure part-writing as such would not be maintained of necessity, as the purpose may be to add to the harmonic rather than contrapuntal interest and effect. But further may we not say if the dominant pedal should persist so as to continue wellnigh to the final cadence, then also Bach would take liberty in accordance with the effect he desired? In other words if the dominant pedal formed a kind of climax, coda or winding up—even though it might be followed by some peroration—it assumed a rôle similar to that more usually filled by the tonic pedal. We see this suggested for example in Vol. II, No. 3, where at the fourth bar from the end is a charmingly decorated dominant pedal. This point one *feels as the climax*, and Bach *does not restrict himself to three strands*. In a sense, Bach indicates that the *fugue proper* is ending, and so liberties may be indulged in.

The tonic pedal following upon this carries the fugue away from this climax to its final repose.

Pedals may be decorated, elaborated as already seen. One cannot refrain from quoting the fine example towards the end of the fugue in E minor, Vol. II, No. 10. The subject in the bass, ending at the third beat, is appropriately continued and brings the six-four on the dominant to fall on the strong beat of the next bar.

This fine specimen of Bach's craftsmanship opens up more than one point; but I will leave it as an instance of the elaboration of a pedal. The student would do himself good service by examining the pedals in all the fugues mentioned so far in this chapter. He should see how Bach approaches and quits them. So often students make a clumsy job of it; they are awkward and spoil the linking up. This dove-tailing has been spoken about earlier in this book; it is always a test of musicianly skill and thought. The student should observe in detail the examples which Bach affords him.

THE FINAL SECTION

The purposes of pedal-points.
The behaviour of voices in stretto above the pedal-point.
Modification of the opening notes of the subject when taking part in stretto.

To many of us a pedal-point is associated with 'closer-stretto', that is, closer than any that may have already occurred in the course of the fugue. Perhaps this has been our only idea of the function of a pedal-point; just a bass note held on while a number of upper voices enter as closely after each other as we can make them (or force them).

Have we been happy in our management of the voices over the pedal? Has their behaviour been musical? Have we been able to continue a voice satisfactorily and with character when overtaken by the next voice? So frequently have I seen a subject, overtaken by the next voice in stretto, suddenly become nondescript and have no further resemblance to the original whatever. Our study will teach us that Bach never *forced* anything. As we look at his fugues we see plainly that the material was always treated as its *nature* suggested; it is when a thing is dealt with *contrary* to its nature that trouble begins. There is no virtue in close entries, unless they occur naturally, unforced. This has been well demonstrated in Chapter X, and the student should glance over this again.

Students often ask if an overtaking voice may be altered so as to make its entry possible. My answer to this question is that although Bach, as we have seen, does not scruple to adapt the opening of his subject to suit a particular moment yet on no occasion, as far as my observation has gone, does he do so to oblige an entry in stretto. Neither the leading nor the overtaking voice may be altered in order to make possible a stretto entry.

A very striking example of freedom in stretto occurs in the fugue in G major, Vol. I, No. 15. Although the function of a pedal-point does not enter much into the matter, yet it calls for comment. From bar 77 onwards Bach appears to abandon himself to his fancy, and to throw all generally accepted precepts to the winds. However, all this would seem to happen *outside* the fugue, when the fugal weaving is *really over*, and *when the coda has set in* (the last full entry of the subject in the tonic key ended in bar 72). This explanation satisfies my own mind about this, and I venture to hope, indicates Bach's attitude regarding it. (We shall refer to this example again.)

Now let us consider some examples of Bach's *Pedal-points*.

The entry at (a) ⌐────┘, Ex. 246, shows the student how Bach modified this theme *immediately* the soprano voice enters. One overlapping note suffices, but although Bach could not follow the *line* of the theme he preserved its rhythmical characteristic. That is the point to which I wish to draw attention here. The chief entry of course is the soprano which

Ex.246

announces the *Answer* (key of the dominant); as yet there is no pedal-point. Note how the pedal note is approached—it is the closing note of a perfect cadence in G. The tenor voice enters over the pedal note and is in stretto to the soprano; not a close stretto, *nor indeed as close as some that have taken place earlier.* But Bach had quite enough happening here, and the entry is more than half a bar after the soprano. Both these voices carry the theme to its full extent. Note that the Tenor does not enter on either the tonic or dominant notes of the key, but on the leading note in C major (or mediant in G major—it does not matter how this is regarded). The theme is treated *diatonically* (note this well) and brings us to a point at the beginning of bar 23 which is no resting place. And what purpose does Bach allow this to serve? He continues, extends it to a full close at the beginning of bar 24 where the fugue could possibly end. *Note that the pedal-point is quitted in quite an unexpected way* giving a touch of F major, the sub-dominant key (bar 22). Yet this example serves to show that stretto may well begin before the pedal-point is reached, a point well worth remembering. From bar 24 to the end is a delightful illustration of a *Tonic-Pedal.* The above quotation leads into it.

Here, over a Tonic Pedal, Bach enjoys the stretto device. The Tenor

Ex.247

is answered at half a bar's distance by the Alto, a fourth above. Both voices make a complete entry—there is no need of any adjustment in the Tenor when overtaken by the Alto. It is delightful to see how Bach plays with the last four semiquavers of the Alto, in bar 25, as a means of extending the music towards its final point of repose—it all seems so simple and apparently inevitable; a perfect peroration.

Vol. I, No. 2, C minor (3 strand).

As in the above C major fugue there is a Tonic Pedal, and Bach, *without any stretto play*, creates a charming and fitting end to the fugue by simply giving the subject to the soprano.

Vol. I, No. 11, F major (3 strands).

In the middle of this fugue, bars 36-40, in the relative minor key, Bach surprises us by introducing a *dominant pedal with voices entering above it in stretto*. The voices run the *full length* of the subject and follow each other at two bars' distance. It is all quite simple to look at. There is no forcing of any sort; the strands go their ways with perfect ease. It is interesting to note how Bach approaches the pedal note—from first inversion of sub-dominant chord—and also how he quits it. I will leave the student to think about such bars as 41-43; they are by no means *ordinary* in their workmanship. How many students would have written them?

Note how the Bass entry is *extended and rounded off* by the perfect cadence at bar 46.

Vol. I, No. 14, F sharp minor (4 strand).

In this smooth flowing fugue we have an ending which in one respect resembles the final section of the C major fugue, Vol. I, No. 1, and in another respect the closing bars of the C minor fugue, Vol. I, No. 2. At bar 37, the fourth from the end, Bach makes the last announcement of this dignified fugal theme which, running its full course, brings the fugue to a noble close. It is like the C major fugue in that this entry of the theme begins *before the dominant pedal is reached.* (Note that it is approached from an inversion of the sub-dominant chord broadly speaking—or to be exact the added sixth.) It is like the C minor fugue in that a simple complete statement of the subject, without any stretto, brings the work to an end. The difference between this F sharp minor and the C minor is that the pedal point in one is Dominant and the other Tonic. Look at these bars; the theme is accompanied by its counter-subject as at first and by another theme all of which occurring over the pedal create a new and culminating effect.

Vol. I, No. 20, A minor (4 strand).

This fugue should be closely studied from bar 73 to the end, but we will confine our attention to those bars following the pause in bar 80. A diminished seventh chord (the chromatic super-tonic minor ninth in A minor) in bar 80 is the approach to the pedal point in bar 81, at first a six-four on the dominant and then dominant seventh.

Before the pedal-point is reached, the Alto voice in bar 80 takes up the subject in the Tonic key; the soprano overtakes it at a half-bar's distance immediately the pedal-point has commenced (as a six-four chord in bar 81). Both these *voices maintain the subject—not the whole of it, but the 'head'.* How amazingly easily and comfortably it all runs and fits in. Neither contrapuntally nor harmonically is there any forcing. Note also how naturally Bach *carries this forward* to the final cadence in bar 83, and from this point to the end is a Tonic Pedal as already mentioned. It is impossible to play these final bars over Tonic pedal, as printed, on the harpsichord or piano. This long tonic sustained note needs the organ pedal.

The Alto version of the subject is correct. The Soprano version is *not an answer* at the fifth above, because it is not in E minor. Bach makes it a response *dominantly* but within the key, and so it is modified. The char-

Ex.251

acteristic leap of a diminished seventh at the end is maintained. This
example shows us the kind of liberty that Bach indulged in. That only
the 'head' of the subject is used and not the whole seems to defy the
generally followed principle of making the full subject appear at such a
point. But even here Bach evidently had weighed matters carefully,
because he stresses this same 'head' of the subject in the final four and a
half bars over the Tonic pedal. He merely insists upon the more arresting
part of the subject and uses it in a properly balanced way. From the pause
(bar 80) to the end (bar 87) is a carefully considered and logical design.

Ex.252

In this long fugue there are many stretti. It might well form a study in
stretto writing. Sometimes the subject in direct form is overtaken by the
subject in direct or inverted form, and so on. Obviously the subject lends
itself to this stretto device and Bach knew it. Once again it serves to impress upon us that Bach did not work on the wrong kind of material, nor did
he attempt to force stretto out of material which could not yield it naturally.

Fugue in C sharp major, Vol. II, No. 3.

Let the student turn to his fugue book. The subject of this particular
example is very short and the two instances of dominant pedal-point
should be examined. One of these has been referred to on page 172,
Ex. 244. Over the tonic pedal in the final bars we see Bach using the subject (merely four-notes) in diminution. These pedal-points show what
can be evolved from very simple or unpretentious material.

Fugue in E minor, Vol. II, No. 10.

This fugue has a long subject. Over the amazing dominant pedal spoken of already on page 172, Ex. 245, there is no stretto. The whole coda of which it forms part is quite a fantasia.

Fugue in G minor, Vol. II, No. 16.

At the fifth bar from the end a Tonic pedal—an inverted-pedal—appears in the soprano voice. Although this is part of the coda—for the fugue's final close in G minor happened at bars 74 to 75—yet we must study it carefully. In the bar previous to this tonic pedal, the theme enters in the Bass. It continues to the end, but is a delightfully elaborated version of the original, and it is a slightly but effectively modified version too. We meet B naturals in place of B flats and they enrich the harmonic effect. The two accompanying strands, alto and tenor, toy with an idea from the first bar of the counter-subject; altogether making a charming texture.

It is somewhat akin to Vol. I, Nos. 1 and 2. Obviously these Tonic and final Pedal points attracted Bach very much. Through them he has given to us moments of great beauty.

In these quotations from the '48' we have seen something of Bach's manner of treating Pedal-points (Dominant and Tonic), over which he sometimes has used stretto device, and sometimes not. We have noted his use of the 'head' of a subject—in this particular instance the more arresting part of the subject—instead of the complete thing. And this too in the final section of the fugue (as distinct from the Coda or peroration) where we have accustomed ourselves to expect a full statement of the subject by the last voice of the stretto. If we regard this as a liberty, we at least realize that Bach carries it through convincingly. But surely it is all musical common sense.

Tonic Pedal-points seem to be associated with the Coda when the weaving of the *fugue proper* is over and the loom is coming to a standstill.

It would seem that 'liberties' are not *generally* taken during the final section as distinct from the Coda. The Coda is the place where Bach relaxes, lets himself go, giving us at times quite startling things. It is therefore important to distinguish the final section from the Coda, to realize where the former finishes. If we do not, we shall fail to appreciate this difference of attitude as demonstrated above, and consequently misjudge his technique. A clear understanding of this compels us to accept the fact that Bach does things *intentionally*, never forgetfully. He made no slips. And apropos of this, I would like to end this short discourse upon Pedal-points by referring to

The Fugue in G major, Vol. I, No. 15.

If we do not realize that the last *true* entry of the subject (in contrary motion too) is concluded in bar 72, and from that point onwards is Coda as distinct from final section, we are likely to conclude that Bach just runs riot here.

For example, we see at bar 77 a dominant Pedal, the subject inverted in the Alto voice and overtaken at bar 79 by the soprano. At first sight we might pass this by without comment, as it seems in perfect order. But on closer examination we discover that the theme in the Alto does not run *truly* as an inverted form should. To be true the fourth quaver E in bar 78 should be G, and the following F sharp should be A. This is a type of modification which I do not find within the fugue *proper* anywhere else, and at once I wonder what Bach is doing. Again at bar 80 the soprano voice *to be true* should have F sharp on the fourth quaver instead of A. This would alter the rest of this presentation of the theme. An explanation of this is necessary. If none is forthcoming, this behaviour of Bach

Ex. 254

is disturbing. But the whole matter becomes clear if we appreciate the difference between the final section which is still the *fugue-proper* and the Coda or peroration. The above happenings occur *during the* process of evolving the Coda of the fugue, and fall *outside* or beyond the fugue proper. Bach's shedding of restraint is thus explained and justified.

A review of Final Section and Coda, incorporating Pedal-point

A. The scheme of Vol. I, No. 1 (4 strand) commends itself in principle and is adaptable.

1. The pedal point is reached after the theme has entered.

2. After the pedal point has been struck, another voice enters in stretto—it runs full length of the theme, extends and reaches a full close.

3. Then follows a peroration over Tonic pedal (see Ex. 247, page 174). Although the final section to the full close after the dominant pedal is not sufficiently long from the point of view of architectural balance this is rectified by the addition of the peroration over the Tonic pedal.

B. The scheme of the pedal point in the middle of Fugue, Vol. I, No. 11, is a clear and attractive three-strand example. It is a longish pedal point. All this could be applied to the final section. If not sufficiently long it might be either further extended or followed by a shortish Tonic pedal.

C. The final section of Vol. I, No. 14, is interesting. It begins in bar 29 with an entry in the Bass, accompanied by its regular counter-subject and a free voice. This is succeeded immediately by the Theme in contrariwise motion still in the Bass with three new counterpoints against it. This is extended in an attractive manner leading to the final entry in the Soprano over a dominant pedal, accompanied by the regular counter-subject and a free strand. This is an attractive scheme for the right kind of subject.

D. Vol. II, No. 10. This final section follows a pause. *One entry* of this long subject in the Bass, accompanied at first by one free voice and then also by another using the regular counter-subject, is sufficient, but it leads to a decorated dominant pedal of considerable length and creates quite a fantasia-like coda. This type is hardly likely to commend itself for examination room work.

E. Vol. II, No. 16. This final section with coda is a delightful scheme of treatment. The coda should be studied. The first three bars of it spring from an idea in the counter-subject. Then follows a final entry of the theme, with *some alterations*, beneath an inverted tonic pedal in the soprano (see Ex. 253, page 178).

The final section begins at bar 67 with the subject and counter-subject. These are overtaken by the theme at the octave together with a counter-subject transferred to the twelfth below. The theme runs its full course and is extended to bar 75 where the coda begins (described above). The texture of this final section is strong and attractive besides being interesting contrapuntally.

The whole scheme commends itself.

Ex.255

Review of Final Section not incorporating any Pedal-point

The following examples it is hoped will afford sufficient variety to help the student in his own work, and provide enough incentive for him to explore among the rest of the '48'.

Fugue in C sharp major, Vol. I, No. 3. This subject is a real one, ending in the Tonic key.

Because of the value of our study of this final section, it is quoted in full. Its comparison with the exposition, episode and redundant Answer occupying the first eleven bars, is to say the least, somewhat enlightening. The student will note that the *exposition is in triple counterpoint.*

The final section from bar 42 shows this in fresh aspects—the voices exchange places—except when the Bass enters in bar 46. In bars 46 and 47 we have an exact restatement of bars 5 and 6 of the exposition. However, so far even there has been *newness.* After this version which ends at bar 48^1 there is a subtle extension to bar 48^3. Only half a bar you may say, but it cannot be left out nor can we pass it over. The episode into which Bach moves does not commence until bar 48^3 (the last two semiquavers of the third beat), and he must link this up with the end of the subject 48^1. Here is a place where a student spoils things—and that is why I draw attention to

it. In the latter half of the bar the Alto responds to the Soprano in the first half and the chain of thought is unbroken. Everything dovetails in, but not by accident. Having reached bar 48^3 we shall observe that the episode following the exposition in bars 7^1-10^1, now recurs in bars 48^3-51^3, but *transposed*. Let us ask, why is it transposed? The answer to this question is of intrinsic importance. We must look ahead a little, and we shall discover the thought behind it all. In the exposition this episodical period led on to a redundant Answer; the fugue being Real, this meant that the dominant key must be reached at that particular point. Now in the final section the corresponding episode leads to a redundant and closing appearance of the *Subject* and must therefore lead to the *Tonic* key. Thus does Bach reveal the sureness of his skill and sense of balance. This exposition and Final section are parallel to the Exposition and Recapitulation of Sonata Form; quite an anticipation of it. This last entry of the subject is prolonged by the same characteristically sure hand, creating music such as 'pleases the mind'.

For the student this is a delightful and no less adaptable scheme. The first episode, whether it leads to a redundant entry or not, could be used as Bach shows us in the final section of this C sharp major fugue.

Fugue in E flat major, Vol. I, No. 7

This subject is a Tonal one, ending in the dominant key. The layout of the exposition and final section in this fugue reflect the procedure of the one just examined. But as its subject is Tonal (whereas the C sharp major one was Real) it will show the student how to carry out the scheme of design.

The following is a kind of skeleton of the Exposition, and it can be compared with the skeleton sketch of the Final section given beneath it.

(The student must have his fugue book open.)

Exposition:

	A	**B**	**C**	**D**	**E**
Subject	C/S in double cpt.		Free strand /////////////		Redundant Answer
(B flat)	Answer	2 strand Codetta	C/S	Episode	Free strand /////////////
	(E flat)		Subject (B flat)		C/S (E flat)

Final section:

	A	**B**	**C**	**D**	**E**	
C/S			Subject (B flat)		New counterpoint \\\\\\\\\\	
Free strand /////////////		3 strand Codetta	C/S	Episode corresponding	Answer—chromatically	Extension
Answer		similar to the above	Free strand /////////////	to the above but varied	altered \\\\\\\\\\	2½ bars
(E flat)					New counterpoint	

The final Section repeats the exposition (apart from the opening statement of the subject), but with full advantage taken of the *double* counterpoint and free strand.

This is a most commendable scheme which the student should find very workable and which does not demand triple counterpoint. He should note the chromatically altered theme in the final entry—Bach here adds a little new colour.

Another example which runs on parallel lines to this E flat major fugue is our oft-quoted *C minor one, Vol. I, No.* 2. A skeleton sketch is given as a guide to the student when making a careful study of the music and its workmanship.

Exposition (the subject is a *real* one in that it remains in its tonic key):

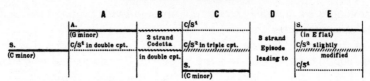

Final Section:

(This is the type of *map* which might be made of a complete fugue and which the student is encouraged to draw.)

Fugue in E major, Vol. I, No. 9

The final section in this follows closely the lines of Vol. I, No. 3 and Vol. I, No. 7. The student should draw skeleton plans of the exposition and final section, he will then see plainly what Bach was doing.

Fugue in F major, Vol. I, No. 11

This final section is rather unusual. Although in the exposition the subject and counter-subject are in double counterpoint, no use of this is made in this final section (merely the slightest suggestion in the middle strand, bar 66). After entries in Stretto in the key of the *super-tonic minor* ending with a full close at bar 56, there is an episode of eight bars. This is really a four-bar phrase in double counterpoint plus a free part, which is repeated showing an interchange (it should be studied in detail). This leads to the entry of the subject which runs its full course accompanied by two free strands. There is only this one entry, slightly extended and rounding off the fugue. The student should refer to this, and also to

Fugue in F sharp major, Vol. I, No. 13

In which a similar design is carried out. Instead of the *super-tonic* minor key, the *sub-dominant major key* is chosen for the entry which occupies the corresponding place.

Fugue in G minor, Vol. I, No. 16

Here is a delightful final section, most satisfying to the musical mind. It is seven bars long; the fugue runs for thirty-four bars. We will examine these seven bars and see if they are remarkable in any way, and if they give us any new ideas for our own work.

Ex.257

In bar 28 we note there is stretto between soprano and tenor, but this half-bar interval is not closer than an earlier stretto in the fugue. This is mentioned to dispel from the student's mind any idea that the final section stretto *must* be at a closer distance than any previous example. Both these voices go the full length of the subject, and there is no adjustment except for the last note of the soprano voice. The stretto is at the *octave* and this is adhered to by all the later entries; no voice overtakes at the answer-level.

What *appears* like a stretto entry occurs in the Bass in bar 29, but at the fourth crotchet its course is adjusted to allow the Tenor to complete its full course. Note that although this Bass entry is adjusted, nevertheless it maintains the rhythmic pattern of the entire subject. This entry is a kind of mock stretto, and obviously has artistic purpose. In bar 28 it will be seen that the Soprano is accompanied by the original counter-subject.

The Tenor at bar 30^1 has run its full course of the subject. How does Bach continue? He uses the little figure ♫♪♫♪ as the basis of this codetta in a manner parallel to that in bar 4, only more is going on. All the voices take part in it now instead of two. This motive or figure becomes in the Bass the true counter-subject in bar 32 against the subject in the Alto. The honour of singing the theme at its last appearance falls to the Tenor. It is accompanied by new free parts making fuller harmonic effect here and there. It gives a dignified close to this lyrical and intimate fugue which is a great favourite.

I am now, with the reader's acquiescence, going to refer to an occurrence just preceding the final section of this fugue, which should prove to be of both interest and value. It falls outside the final section proper, but leads up to it. If we turn back to bar 20 we shall there find a Bass entry of the theme in the key of the sub-dominant minor, and when this has run its full course, another such entry occurs in the soprano, bar 21. Both these entries are accompanied by the original counter-subject, or to be exact, the *regular* portion of it which occurs after the adjustment of the tonal Answer (this is a point not to be overlooked).

At bar 23 we meet the occasion to which I would draw attention. At this point, in the Alto, the Answer to these sub-dominant entries appears. This is of course the theme in the tonic key of G minor with the slight tonal alteration at the outset as it is a proper tonal response to the C minor entry. It is accompanied by the regular counter-subject and a free part. *Now this response in the tonic key comes to a perfect cadence in bar 24³, but as yet we have not reached the final section of the fugue. It is at such a point that the student is often uncertain what to do.* How does Bach go forward with his design? He creates an episode which adds harmonic colour, but returns to G minor, its starting-point. By sequential treatment of the familiar figure ♫♪♫♪ he builds this episode which has freshness (note the two upper strands) and which comes to a close on dominant harmony in bar 28¹. Here the final section opens up.

The study of this sub-dominant and later portion of the fugue should be a model lesson, to which no doubt the student will refer many times.

Fugue in C minor, Vol. II, No. 2

This final section illustrates *augmentation of the theme*.

With regard to this particular treatment of a fugal theme we shall see

once more that Bach never forced the situation. He always chose most wisely the occasions when he brought into play this or that fugal device, and so he never produced awkwardness. The smooth weaving of the design was not spoiled, because the nature of the material suited the process. If the student will allow the nature of his material to guide him, he will be spared much disappointment. There are many 'marvellous places' in the '48' which take one's breath away by their very skilfulness. We are humbled in the presence of such contrapuntal technique. But these places can also be an encouragement to us if we remember that they are the outcome of 'the right thing done at the right time', the result of 'the treatment of material according to its nature'.

As this final section has points of similarity with the G minor one just considered, it is quoted in full, so that the student may compare them at his leisure.

A first glance at bars 19 and 20 does not reveal any special point of technique, but I think that Bach has used a semblance of the subject in the soprano. Bar 20 seems to be a working towards the cadence without any particular device beyond a little imitation between the Alto and Soprano. Nevertheless the ♪♪♪♪ group in bar 19 is subtly maintained all the way along as far as the final cadence in bar 23. I think too that as Bach has indulged considerably in stretto in bars 16, 17, 18, he considered there had been sufficient of it. This to my mind is borne out by the fact that in bars 21 and 22 the subject matter is kept in the Bass and there is no device. Further, the close stretti appear with all the more freshness in the coda. It must be remembered too that already Bach has shown the *theme in augmentation* combined with the theme itself in two astonishing bars which must be quoted. They need no comment beyond the one fact that they illustrate Bach's ever alert mind.

Ex.259

Fugue in D sharp minor, Vol. I, No. 8

This fugue shows the use of *augmentation in the course of its expansion as well as at the final section*. The student should not fail to study from bar 62 to the end, but here we must be content with the quotation of the great winding-up section only.

Here again we see the master-mind at work, but it is not merely a display of skill. The alto line beginning in bar 77 shows how a little *metamorphosis of theme* can play its part. Look at bar 83 onwards to the end. What a wonderful ending Bach evolves! By what means? By nothing

Ex.260

more than the musicianly use of the figure at a ⌐———⌐ (bar 77) taken from the subject. Examine in detail this superb example of the treatment of material *according to its nature*.

The Pause and its significance

A pause in music usually indicates a point of significance towards which the composer has been working. It does not necessarily coincide with a peak-point of tone power; it may occur later on, at a place where the tone power has considerably receded from its high point. In any case, it marks a climax of some kind, and begets a sense of wonder in the listener's mind as to what will happen next.

For instance, in the Fugue in E minor (Vol. I, No. 10) a pause occurs in the fourth bar from the end. It would seem as if the exciting activity which has been going on over the dominant-pedal has spent itself and demands a little respite. The pause affords this, and in doing so, serves another purpose. It emphasizes the rounding off of the whole fugue, realized in the immediate resumption of the activity which is characteristic of this fantasia-like Coda. In all this one cannot fail to appreciate the effectiveness of the pause both musically and psychologically.

At bar 70 in this Fugue, the psychological attribute of the pause is perhaps more markedly shown. At this point a state of repose has been gradually reached; the mind is willing to linger restfully. But what next? It is suddenly awakened by the arresting passage of triplet-quavers which in a flash leads to the imposing announcement of the final appearance of the subject, in the Bass. Thus is greater significance given to this long fugal theme. Bach understood the power of the pause.

Other instances occur in the Fugue in A minor (Vol. I, No. 20) and in the Fugue in A flat major (Vol. II, No. 17). In the former, at the pause in bar 80, a great crescendo has culminated. Will the tension be relieved? That is the listener's thought during the suspense created by this prolonged chord. Bach does *not* relax the strain; rather does he intensify it. Not only is the tone strength maintained but its forcefulness is emphasized by the nature of the next chord, a diminished seventh, and by reason of the unexpectedness of the harmonic progression. Added to this, the immediate and dynamic entry of the fugue subject surely provides a convincing instance of the psychological and dramatic power of the pause.

In the following excerpt taken from the Fugue in A flat (Vol. II, No. 17)

the student will see an example closely resembling the one in the E minor Fugue mentioned above. It is quoted, however, for other reasons too.

Consider the magnetic drive towards the pause as the music passes through bars 44, 45 and 46. What range and resource of harmonic imagination is revealed here! Further, a short sweeping bravura passage launches the subject and its counter theme which continue their course together to the end of the fugue. They move unerringly along in the midst of complex five-strand texture. Could anyone desire a more skilful and satisfying example of contrapuntal art?

Other bravura passages there are in these inexhaustible '48' fugues, of more brilliance than the one just mentioned. The student should look at the fugue in G major, Vol. II, No. 15, and also at the A minor, Vol. II, No. 20.

Of Bach's contrapuntal power at its height one might quote many instances, but possibly none more impressive than the winding-up of the fugue in B flat minor, Vol. II, No. 22. Here we meet with the device known as 'added thirds'. Furthermore, as if Bach were not content with this, he shows us an example of stretto at one beat's distance, with the subject (in added thirds too) in inverted form! Here again there is no forcing. Bach knew and respected the nature of his material, that is all. This is one of the great lessons we, as students, have to learn from him.

Ex. 262

Needless to add, such things as the above are not expected in an examination fugue.

.   .   .   .

The study of Fugue cannot be continued to its full close in a book so short as this. Therefore I would not have the student imagine that this work sets the perimeter line round about his fugal studies. I hope it may incite him to wider exploration of fugue as a means of EXPRESSION. One of the amazing things about the '48' is that Bach's inspiration appears not to be hampered by the practical limitation imposed by ten fingers and a keyboard. If we turn to his organ masterpieces we shall see how his 'expression in fugue' was affected by being able to *think* in terms of not only ten fingers, but also two feet and more than one keyboard. What great creations he has bequeathed to us in this sphere of organ music! Many since Bach's day have worked in it, but few have added to his legacy. Obviously then, there is much outside the '48' for the student to browse over. In time he may discover that the creation of a potential fugue subject is an art of its own. This should impress him and cause him to think about the *nature* of the musical idea we call a fugue subject. It is of no small importance; for a fugue, to be *pleasing to the mind*, cannot be woven from poor material; nor can it be created by treating even good material contrary to its nature. To my mind this explains the many dull fugues which have been written.

Bach's fugues please the mind and satisfy it completely.

Thomas Carlyle on a certain occasion wrote:

'The most profitable employment any book can give us, is to study honestly some earnest, deep-minded, truth-loving man, to work our way into his manner of thought, till we see the world with his eyes, feel as he felt, and judge as he judged, neither believing nor denying till we can in some measure so feel and judge.'

I hope this little book in the cause of Fugue may encourage many a student 'to work his way into the manner and thought' of that deep-minded and truth-loving man John Sebastian Bach. I could wish for no greater reward.

BIBLIOGRAPHY

Spitta, *The Life of Bach* (three volumes.) (Novello & Co., Ltd.)
Parry, *John Sebastian Bach*. (Putnam.)
Schweitzer, *J. S. Bach* (two volumes). (Black.)
Forkel, *Johann Sebastian Bach*. (Constable.)
Grace, *The Organ Works of Bach*. (Novello & Co., Ltd.)
C. S. Terry, *Bach—an Historical Approach*. (Oxford University Press.)
Gray, *Bach's Forty-eight*. (Oxford University Press.)
Wesley, *Bach Letters*. (W. Reeves.)
Taylor, *The Chorale Preludes of J. S. Bach*. (Oxford University Press.)
Dickinson, *The Art of Bach*. (Duckworth.)
Prout, *Fugue*. (Augener.)
Kitson, *Studies in Fugue*. (Oxford University Press.)
Kitson, *The Elements of Fugal Construction*. (Oxford University Press.)
Bairstow, *Counterpoint and Harmony*. (MacMillan & Co., Stainer & Bell.)
Morris, *The Structure of Music*. (Oxford University Press.)
Tovey, *Musical Textures*, and *A Musician Talks* (Oxford University Press.)
Bach, *The Forty-eight Preludes and Fugues*.
The Organ Works of Bach.
Bach, *Two-part and Three-part Inventions*.
E. J. Dent, *Notes on Fugue for Beginners*.
Stewart Macpherson, *Studies in the Art of Counterpoint*. (Joseph Williams.)
Cherubini, *Counterpoint and Fugue*. (Novello & Co., Ltd., 1854.)
Eric Gill, *Art*. (The Bodley Head.)
Maritain, *Art and Scholasticism*. (Sheed & Ward.)
Percy C. Buck, *Unfigured Harmony*. (Oxford University Press.)
J. H. Arnold, *Plainsong Accompaniment*. (Oxford University Press.)
Peter Warlock, *Fantasias for Strings* (1680) *by Henry Purcell*. (J. Curwen & Sons, Ltd.)

The actual works consulted include examples by Palestrina, Andrea Gabrieli, Tallis, Byrd, Mundi, Purcell, Phillips, Morley, Frescobaldi, Pasquini, Pollaroli, Durante, D. Scarlatti, Porpora, Martini, Handel and others.

A COURSE OF STUDY

To the student preparing for examination, the need of some such lay-out plans as were broadly drawn up in Chapter I is all the more emphasized by the substance of the later chapters of this book. We have seen the amazing diversity which is brought about by the treatment of fugue subjects *according to their nature* (nothing being *forced*), combined with the appreciation of architectural and tonal balance. These are the essentials which create the true design of each fugue and which make it a 'particular' work.

Obviously no two subjects will expand on exactly the same lines, because their natures differ from each other. Therefore whatever plan or lay-out is decided upon and followed out, must be regarded and valued, at first, as providing technical experience. Even the results of weaving a subject into a complete design previously decided upon, quite apart from whether or not by nature it is suited to follow such a scheme, need not be frowned upon. Such training offers scope for developing individual insight and for revealing places where improvement may be made. Let us be sure therefore that however far from the ideal as *composition in fugue* the following studies may be in themselves, nevertheless they offer essential service towards the attainment of that ideal. As the student's technique and mastery expand he may feel able to incorporate in his examination fugue more and more of the ideas he has seen so perfectly demonstrated in the work of Bach.

The following example of a complete fugue in three strands may give the student some idea of how a broad, general lay-out may actually work in practice. The lay-out is as short as one could choose, but will perhaps serve our purpose just as well as a longer one. It is the outcome of dealing with a pupil's work. It has not been written specially for this book, but is one of many that might have been inserted at this point. It should be used by the student not as a model of 'the thing to do and copy' but (to quote the pupil's own words) rather as a kind of measuring rod.

Here is the *broad* lay-out previously decided upon:

(a) Exposition with short codettas if necessary, particularly between Answer and Subject. The Subject and Counter-subjects to form triple counterpoint.

(b) First Episode, showing double counterpoint with interchange within its own ground. Possible extension.

(c) One set of middle entries in the relative minor key. Two strands to enter with the theme, which may or may not show slight stretto, accompanied by a third strand. An interchanged version of the triple counterpoint of the exposition to be incorporated.

(d) Second Episode, showing dove-tailing canon. Possible extension.

(e) Final section incorporating stretti and new interchange of the triple counterpoint of the exposition; possibly short dominant pedal, and Coda over Tonic pedal.

Fugue in three strands for strings (written in short score).

It should be pointed out that this three-strand work of the exposition having only just got under way might well be extended a little. This would also provide a rather longer stretch in the home keys. It is this matter regarding the home keys which is important. Often Bach either had good Codetta space or followed the exposition by an episode leading to a redundant entry of either Subject or Answer. These served the same purpose. As I have hinted at extension I will make a suggestion by writing bars 14a, 14b, 14c.

As these bars stand they are open to criticism on the ground that the figure in the bass loses force by occurring four times. It will be noticed that the violin line is not open to such criticism because the figure becomes varied. Some similar treatment might well be applied to the 'cello part thus:

And now for the first Episode, starting either from bar 15 or 14d. The first thing is to sketch the possible basis for passing from E flat major to its relative minor key in which the next entry of the subject will appear.

As we are planning to show interchange within the episode we adopt the sequential idea. If we wish for a slightly longer episode we should choose A, though the scheme B could be extended, carried forward appropriately as indicated by the crosses.

The thing now is to decide upon some figure arising from the material of the exposition. Let us try (x) from the bass of bars 13 and 14. (This has not been worked before, so these ideas have not been tried out.)

This may stand as it is in two strands; or the alto may indulge in a little

195

responsive chatter here and there as hinted by the small notes, which certainly should be done if bars 14a to 14d have not been incorporated.

Both cases illustrate the thinning-out effect, to which attention has been frequently drawn. It is akin to the C minor fugue by Bach (Vol. I, No. 2).

It will be noticed that Y▬▬▬ keeps only the *rhythm* of the previous bars of the exposition, but is *suggestive* of the contour. The point is that it maintains the *spirit* without keeping the letter. There could also be a 'thin' third strand, as in scheme A.

Now introduce the set of *Middle entries in C minor*. If possible make use of slight stretto. If this is not possible do without stretto.

During the first entry of the Subject, work against it some germ or idea from the episode just ended. Let this appear to continue its activity, and finally merge into one of the *counter-subjects* at a suitable place after the second entry. This second entry may be at either the subject-pitch or answer-pitch. The remaining strand will take up the other counter-subject at a suitable point also. Thus:

Set of Middle entries

Episode II.

Now follows the second episode which will illustrate dove-tailing canon. For the purpose of providing *colour* we might touch upon F minor and A♭ major (the sub-dominant key).

Remember that this episode has to lead back to the final section with its balancing stretch of home-tonality.

Sketch out the harmonic route and so provide a basis. Upon this framework, weave a little pattern from some thread taken from one of the strands of the exposition.

Now follows the Final Section

Here we must bear in mind architectural and tonal balance. The length and tonality of this final section must be a satisfying counter-part to the exposition.

As to plan, Chapter XII has shown many. Consider the type of subject and decide to try the broad lay-out of one such section. Be prepared to *modify* such a plan to suit the *nature* of your own subject.

I will try stretto, extension, final entry, and possibly a coda over Tonic pedal.

Here is another three-strand fugue for strings, mainly the work of a pupil. There is no pedal, but the final section shows a build-up to a climax, with coda evidently beyond the fugue proper. I leave the student to make his own observations and comments.

* The fugue could end at bar 48, in which case I should play D flat (shown in brackets) on the first beat of bar 45. The fugue could also be prolonged effectively to bar 50, in which case I should play D natural, not D flat, on the first beat of bar 45, because it would detract somewhat from the effect in bar 48.

The small notes in the Alto of bars 32 and 33 are optional.

Note the freshness of the new harmonic treatment in bar 36; also the colouring during the extension, bars 37, 38, and 39.

A COURSE OF STUDY

Examples of four-strand fugues are given on pages 215 and 218.

Studies with reference to Chapter III—the Counter-subject

To the following themes, write counter-themes forming double counterpoint. The student should write his counter-themes within a range of *two octaves* above or below the given themes. That is, they are interchangeable at the fifteenth, *and the interchanged version should be shown in each case.*

TWO-PART EXERCISES

No. 1. Add a higher part in quavers.

No. 2. Add a higher part in quavers.

No. 3. Starting as follows add a lower part maintaining semiquaver movement. End in F major.

No. 4. Add a lower part mostly in quavers. Use a rest or two.

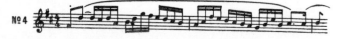

No. 5. Add a lower part in semiquavers.

No. 6. Add a higher part in quavers.

No. 7. Add a lower part in quavers. Let it be different from No. 6.

No. 8. Add a lower part entirely in semiquavers.

No. 9. Add a lower part in semiquavers, except in the final bar.

No. 10. Add a higher part.

No. 11. Add a higher part in quavers.

No. 12. Add a lower part not necessarily in semiquavers.

No. 13. Add a higher part.

No. 14. (C minor) Add a higher part in semiquavers as far as indicated.

No. 15. Add a lower part mostly in quavers.

No. 16. Add a lower part.

No. 17. Add a lower part, maintaining the character as suggested.

No. 18. Add a higher part making an appropriate counter-subject.

No. 19. Add a higher part making an appropriate counter-subject.

No. 20. Add a higher part moving mostly in crotchets.

THREE-PART EXERCISES

A. Two strands forming double counterpoint, plus a free strand.

Exercises

To all the exercises, Nos. 1-20, already worked in two strands forming double counterpoint add a third strand *free*.

B. Two strands forming double counterpoint, plus a third strand forming *Triple counterpoint*. First add a strand forming double counterpoint before adding the third strand. This ensures that the subject and its counter-subject make good two-part harmony.

Note.—Every exercise should be written out showing each strand in the bass.

No. 21. Below this theme add another in double counterpoint. Then add another theme *above* it forming triple counterpoint.

No. 22. Above this theme add another in double counterpoint. Then add another theme (above) forming triple counterpoint.

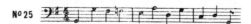

No. 23. Add two themes above this Bass, forming triple counterpoint.

No. 24. Add two themes below this melody, forming triple counterpoint.

No. 25. Add two themes above the Bass, forming triple counterpoint. Delay the entry of the middle voice until the eighth quaver of the first bar. Let the uppermost voice be mainly in semiquavers, and the middle voice employ quavers mostly and a few rests.

No. 26. Add two upper parts, forming triple counterpoint.

No. 27. Add an upper part in semiquavers and a lower part in crotchets, forming triple counterpoint.

No. 28. Above the following Bass add a Soprano of instrumental range. Let the first **bar** be in quavers, and the remainder mostly semiquavers.

No. 29. To the Bass and Soprano worked together in No. 28, add a middle strand. Let the first bar move in semiquavers. The remainder in varied lengths of notes. It should form triple counterpoint. (Show the interchanged versions.)

No. 30. To the given Bass add an instrumental Alto strand, forming double counterpoint.

Then add a Soprano strand, forming triple counterpoint.

No. 31. Above this Bass add an Alto of vocal range, forming double counterpoint.

Then add a Soprano strand, forming Triple counterpoint.

No. 32. Add an instrumental Alto below this subject, forming double counterpoint.

Then add an instrumental Bass, forming triple counterpoint.

No. 33. To the given subject for viola, add a 2nd violin, forming double counterpoint.

Then add a 1st violin, forming triple counterpoint.

No. 34. Below this violin subject write a counter-subject (at the fifteenth) for 'cello.

Then add a 2nd violin part, forming triple counterpoint.

No. 35. Above this 'cello subject write a counter-subject (at the fifteenth) for 2nd violin.

Then add a 1st violin part, forming triple counterpoint.

No. 36. To the following subject add an appropriate Alto, forming double counterpoint.

Then add a Soprano, forming triple counterpoint.

No. 37. To the following subject add an appropriate counter-subject below. Then add a free part above or a part forming triple counterpoint.

No. 38. To the following subject add an appropriate counter-subject below in double counterpoint. Start as suggested.

No. 39. Add your counter-subject of No. 38 to the following tonal reply, and continue the soprano strand to form triple counterpoint. The upper parts may cross.

No. 40. To the foilowing subject for 'cello add a viola part, forming double counterpoint. Then add a violin part, forming triple counterpoint.

Studies with reference to Chapter IV. The Codetta

CASE I. Between the last note of the following subjects and the entry of the Answer, add a short link or codetta.

(a) *Codetta made by extending the ending of the subject.*
The next entry to be given to the viola as indicated.

No. 42. The next entry to be given to the viola as indicated.

(b) *Codetta made by using an idea occurring in the early or middle part of the subject.*

No. 43. The next entry to be given to the viola as indicated.

No. 44. The next entry to be given to the viola as indicated.

No. 45. The next entry to be given to the viola as indicated.

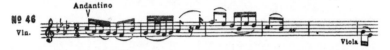

(c) *Codetta made from new material, having affinity with the subject.*
No. 46. The next entry to be given to the viola as indicated.

No. 47. The next entry to be given to the violin as indicated.

(d) *To the following add your own codetta as you consider appropriate.*

CASE II. The codetta between the Answer and the second appearance of the subject.

The following themes are ANSWERS to subjects.

The student should first of all add an appropriate counter-subject to each one, then add a codetta leading to the entry of the subject in the Tonic key.

In writing these codettas, he should apply one or other of the methods found on pages 46 *et seq.*, choosing and trying out the type which he, in his judgment, considers most suitable.

As the student will have similar decisions to make in every fugal exposition he attempts, it is obvious that much further practice in the matter of codettas will be afforded him when he works the exercises provided in the later part of this book.

Studies with reference to Chapter V. The Answer

Bearing in mind CLASSES II, III and IV mentioned on page 53, and fully discussed in Chapter V, let the student answer the following subjects. He should be able to justify his procedure.

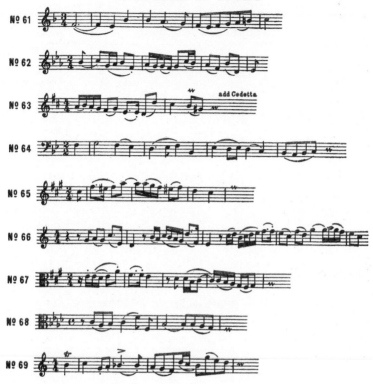

No. 70. To the following subject write the Answer and to this add a counter-subject.

Then compare yours with Bach's working (Vol. II, No. 17). Add a short codetta of one and a half bars to the given subject.

No. 71. Add a short link so that the Answer may enter on the second quaver of the next bar.

No. 72. Add a suitable link leading to the entry of the Answer. Show the Answer in the Alto.

A COURSE OF STUDY

No. 73. Continue the Answer, adding Counter-subject. Then extend suitably before bringing in the subject again.

No. 74. Continue the Answer.

No. 75. Add the Answer and Counter-subject.

Answer the following subjects:

No. 82. The following subject should be answered by the student. *Then*, he should look up Bach's Fugue in E minor and make comparisons. Bach's Answer should not be viewed without studying the full context.

The student will have further material upon which to exercise his judgment in the studies which are provided in connexion with the later chapters of the book.

Studies with reference to Chapter VI. The Exposition

In writing Expositions the student should bear in mind the numerous observations mentioned in Chapter VI.

1. He should consider whether the Answer will come above or below the continuation of the subject, that is the counter-subject.

2. He should apply the methods of writing counter-subjects in Double and Triple Counterpoint. He should practise adding a counter-subject in Double Counterpoint, and to this another one which is quite free; or one which will form Triple Counterpoint.

3. He should pursue each strand throughout the whole exposition as illustrated in examples 145, 146, 147.

He should consider each strand as a continuous thing making a satisfactory musical line. It must not be an incoherent patch-work.

The strands in combination should create a good, balanced texture in which all have their fair share.

4. He should avoid the error of not allowing equal opportunity to the last added strand to play its part in the texture.

5. He should be alive to the value of codetta spaces for providing potential material.

THREE-STRAND EXPOSITIONS

Upon the following Fugue subjects the student should write expositions by

(a) Adding a Counter-subject in double counterpoint, and another as a free strand.

(b) Adding a Counter-subject in double counterpoint and another forming triple counterpoint.

No. 83. For Violin, Viola and 'Cello.

No. 84. For 'cello, viola and violin, or organ.

No. 85. For 'cello, viola and violin.

No. 86. For 'cello, viola and violin.

No. 87. For violin, viola and 'cello.

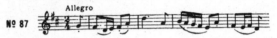

No. 88. For 'cello, viola and violin.

No. 89. For strings.

No. 90. For strings.

No. 91. For strings.

No. 92. For strings.

No. 93. For strings.

A COURSE OF STUDY

No. 94. For strings.

FOUR-STRAND EXPOSITIONS

No. 95. Strings.

No. 96. Strings.

No. 97. Strings.

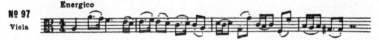

No. 98. Organ.

No. 99. Strings.

No. 100. Strings.

No. 101. Strings.

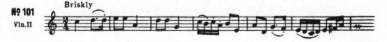

No. 102. Strings.

No. 103. Strings:

No. 104. Organ or strings.

Studies with reference to Chapters VII-XII

After writing the Expositions set in Chapter VI, the student should now continue them and gradually extend them into complete fugues.

He can follow whatever method he finds best. For instance he may add the first episode to each exposition already worked, in order to get practice with this particular section of the fugue. This should develop his power of creating variety. In this way he may complete the fugues step by step. Generally speaking this is quite a wise procedure, but some students may care to attempt the completion of each fugue in turn, but I do not advise this at the outset.

As to the lay-out, he may find it profitable at first to keep to a stereo-typed one. In this way his mind is likely to gain speed in working and a sense of confidence. Having achieved a measure of skill the student will undoubtedly desire to create fugues which break away from the stereo-typed plan, and employ more and more of the mind of Bach.

An example of a fugue worked by a student following the original lay-out using three episodes is now given. It is a four-strand fugue, but of course the lay-out may be used in three-strand workings. Finally, a D.Mus. fugue is given, worked by a student on the two-episode plan. In studying these and the earlier specimens provided in this course the student should remember that they are merely 'measuring rods' to help him to assess his own work.

FUGUE FOR STRING QUARTET

FUGUE FOR STRING QUARTET

D.Mus.(Lond) 1944

A COURSE OF STUDY

1st Episode, triple Cpt. with interchange